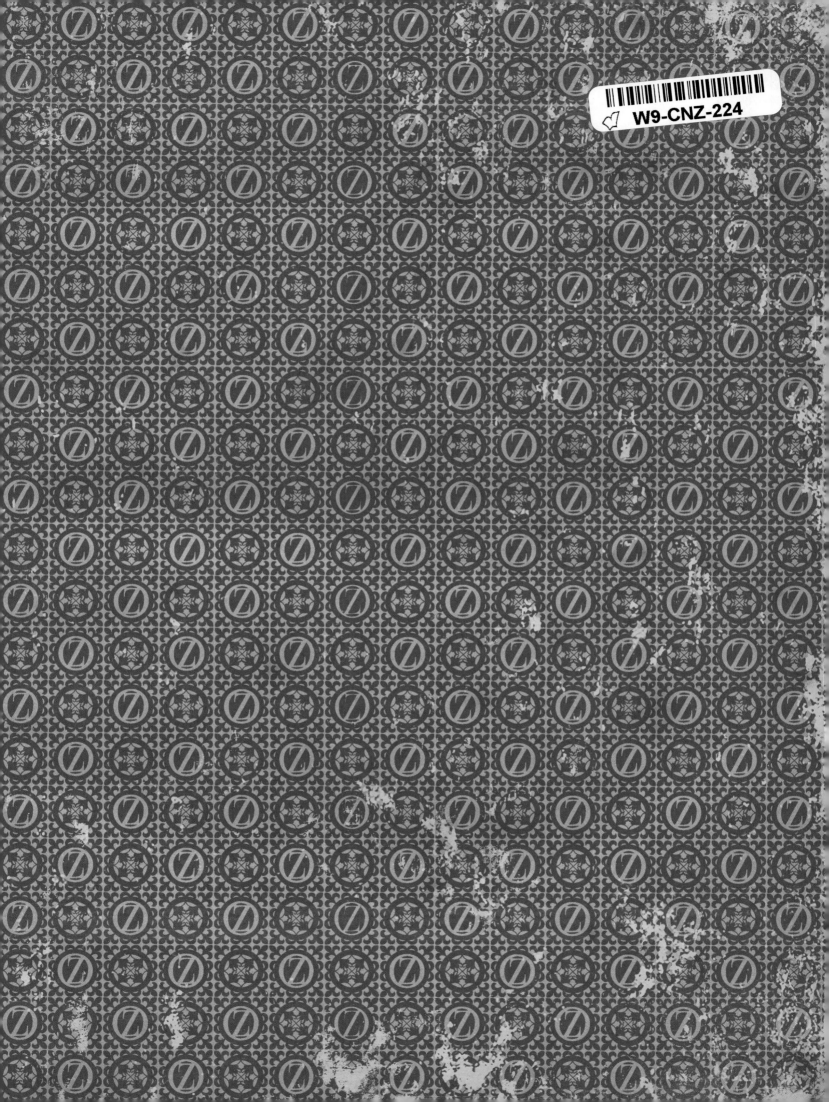

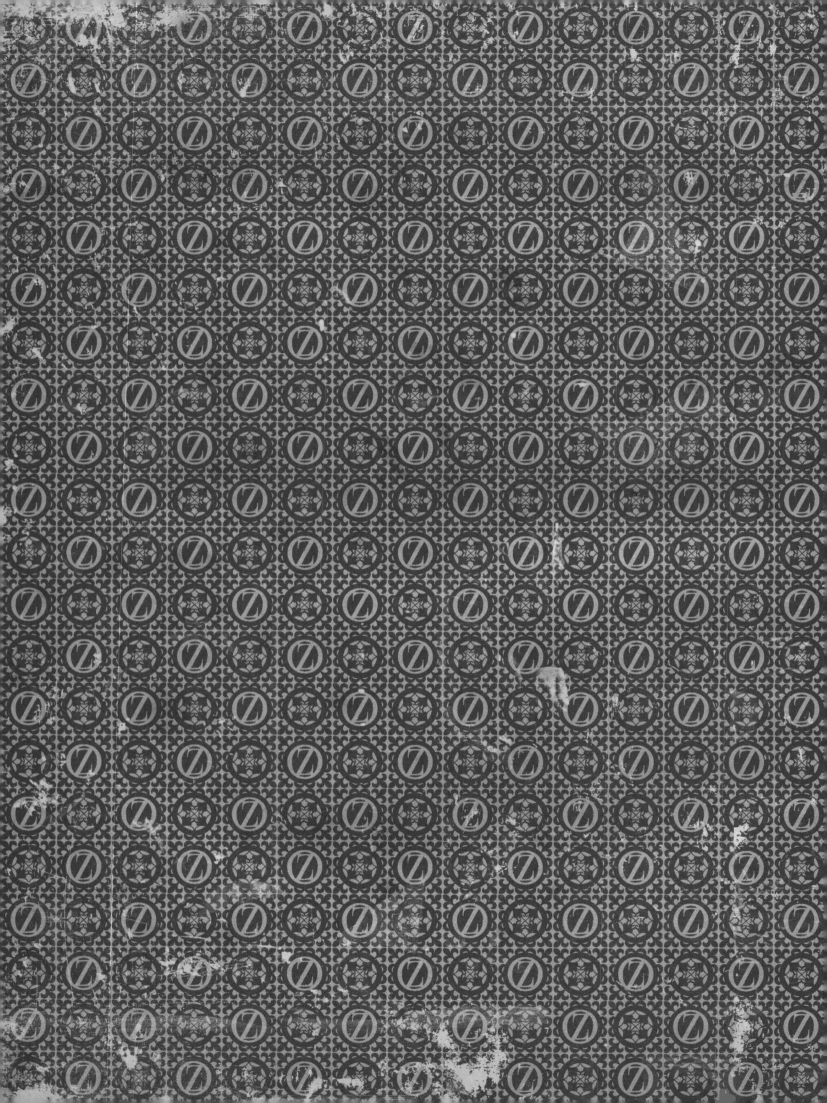

BEHOLD, A GRIMMERIE:

In my novel *Wicked: The Life and Times of the Wicked Witch of the West*, I named Elphaba's book of spells a Grimmerie. I conjured up the word Grimmerie to prompt associations of several things at once: of the Brothers Grimm, with their tales of magic and witches and forests; of grimness itself. But also I meant slyly to echo the archaic word *gramarye*. The Oxford English Dictionary defines *gramarye* as "occult learning, magic, necromancy." There is a solid philological relationship to the Scottish word glamour—the casting of a spell over the eyes of a spectator . . .

—GREGORY MAGUIRE,
Massachusetts, 2005

WICKED

The
GRIMMERIE

Text & Interviews by

DAVID COTE

*Principal Photography by**Designed by*

JOAN MARCUS ⁂ HEADCASE DESIGN

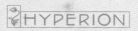HYPERION | MELCHER MEDIA

Published by
HYPERION
114 Fifth Avenue, New York, NY 10011-5604

Produced by
MELCHER MEDIA
124 West 13th Street, New York, NY 10011, www.melcher.com

© 2005 WICKED LLC
Text by DAVID COTE
Principal Photography by JOAN MARCUS
Design by HEADCASE DESIGN, www.headcasedesign.com
The Songs and Story of *Wicked* by STEPHEN SCHWARTZ and WINNIE HOLZMAN
Songs and Lyrics by STEPHEN SCHWARTZ
Abridged Story by WINNIE HOLZMAN
Acknowledgments, additional copyright information, photography and other credits,
constituting an extension of the copyright page, appear on page 192.

First Edition
13 12   10 9 8

Printed in China

ISBN: 978-1-4013-0820-9
Library of Congress Control Number: 2005927456

SO MUCH HAPPENED BEFORE
DOROTHY DROPPED IN . . .

WARNING TO ALL READERS:
There are Spoilers afoot. Proceed with Caution.

TABLE of CONTENTS

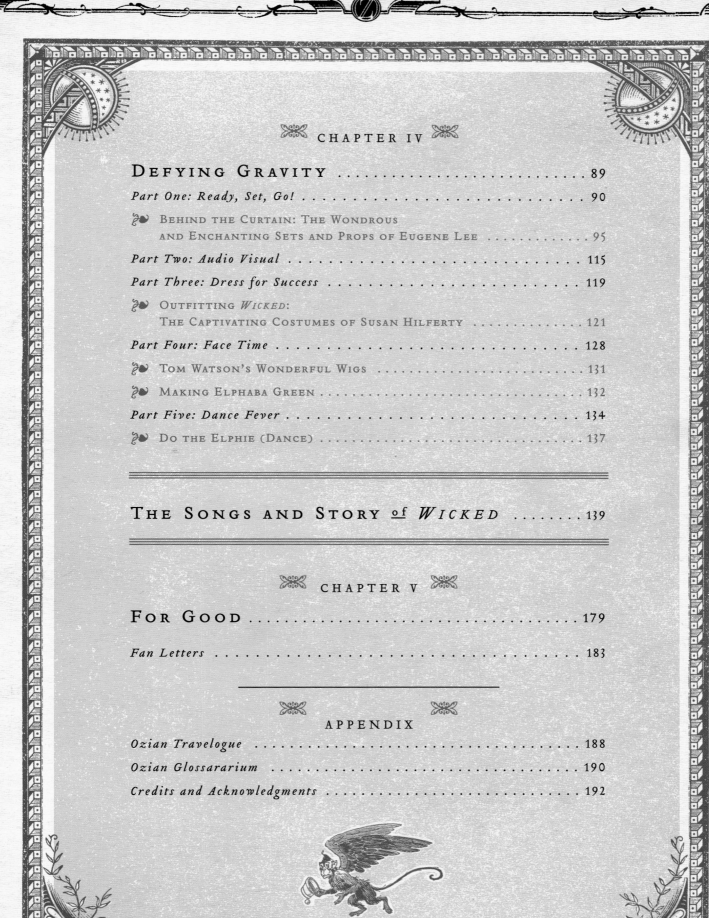

FOREWORD

by Marc Platt

 **E**VER SINCE I WAS A KID, I DREAMED ABOUT WORKING IN THE THEATER. WHEN I SET OUT PROFESSIONALLY, THE ONE THING I WANTED TO DO ABOVE ALL ELSE WAS TO PRODUCE A BROADWAY MUSICAL. THEN SOMEHOW, BY AN UNEXPECTED TWISTER OF FATE, I took a left turn into the film business. Before I knew it, I was the president of a motion picture studio, three thousand miles from Broadway and making movies. Little did I know in June of 1996, the first time I read Gregory Maguire's brilliant and compelling novel *Wicked: The Life and Times of the Wicked Witch of the West*, that this book would be the vehicle that would enable me to realize my dream and would change me—for good.

Coming from the world of film, I initially envisioned *Wicked* as a movie. Thankfully, Stephen Schwartz convinced me that creating *Wicked* as a stage musical would give this story its richest fulfillment. He was right.

Through Stephen's captivating score and insightful lyrics, Winnie Holzman's witty and clever book, and Joe Mantello and his creative team's imaginative and innovative staging and design, *Wicked* transports audiences to a magical land as it uniquely reinvents the world of Oz and the beloved Frank Baum characters. Yet beyond the enchantment, fun, and delight of watching familiar characters take unexpected turns, *Wicked* explores ideas and themes that resonate throughout time.

As Elphaba and Glinda journey through Oz, they develop the courage to accept the differences between them, to take responsibility for the power they have earned or been given, and to understand the true and transcendent meaning of friendship. *Wicked* explores the nature of good and evil and allows us to understand how politics, history, and circumstance conspire to create misplaced labels— and how those labels distort the way we view the past and inform the way we approach the future.

Every time I see *Wicked*, I am struck by the enormity of the production and I remain awed by the vision, talent, and tenacity that our creative team, management group, cast, and crew brought to this venture. *Wicked* was the fruition of so much hard work by so many remarkably gifted people both in front of the curtain and behind. Yet throughout this wonderful journey, nothing has compared to experiencing the audience's response to *Wicked*. I am overwhelmed by the nightly standing ovations and thunderous applause, the rock-concert style enthusiasm during every performance, the fans who have gone to see the show time and time again, and the constant comments from people telling me that they can't stop listening to the original cast recording because they love the music so much. It is my hope that this book will capture some of those memories and bring our audience behind the scenes with us to see how we built our yellow brick road from novel to Broadway.

OZ WELL THAT ENDS WELL

The stars of Wicked *pose for photographer Henry Leutwyler on September 8, 2003. {*FROM LEFT*} Carole Shelley as Madame Morrible, Kristin Chenoweth as Glinda, Manuel Herrera as Chistery, Joel Grey as the Wonderful Wizard of Oz, Idina Menzel as Elphaba, and Norbert Leo Butz as Fiyero*

THE ROAD TO WICKED

MAY 1891:

Baum and his family move to Chicago after difficult days in South Dakota, where both his store (Baum's Bazaar) and newspaper (*The Aberdeen Saturday Pioneer*) prove unsuccessful. He works as a reporter for *The Chicago Evening Post* and then becomes a traveling salesman for a china dishware company. To while away the hours on the road, he fashions nonsense verse and fairy tales; whenever he's home, these rhymes and stories entrance his wife and four growing sons (above, from left: Robert, Harry, Kenneth, and Frank, with Maud), as well as neighborhood children.

MAY 15, 1900:

On Baum's 44th birthday, his n collaboration with Denslow, *The Wonderful Wizard of Oz,* rolls off the printing presses wi more than 100 line illustrations 24 full-color plates. At $1.50 pe it becomes another and immed bestseller. Baum starts to receiv ardent fan letters from his you readers; by December—accordi family legend—the author is astounded when he asks his pu for an advance on royalties for Christmas shopping and receiv first payment of $3,432.64. (She here, an early reprint. Note the tive has been dropped from the

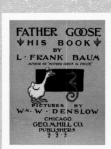

1882:

Baum's abiding love of the theater leads him to blithely write script, lyrics, and music for *The Maid of Arran*, "an Irish Idyll." He also plays the lead male role—Hugh Holcomb, "a fair-haired stranger"—in this whimsical melodrama. The play is a hit with both audiences and critics and tours the country for several seasons. The same year, Baum falls in love with and marries Maud Gage, daughter of noted feminist Matilda Joslyn Gage.

MAY 15, 1856:

Lyman Frank Baum is born in Chittenango, New York, east of Syracuse. He grows up a frail child with a weak heart (the ailment will plague him his entire life) but an active imagination. He dislikes his first name and prefers to go by Frank. Physically restricted due to his medical condition, the young Baum spends his playtime devouring novels by Dickens and Thackeray, as well as English fairy tales, in his father's study; it is there, immersed in those volumes, that he discovers his own passion for writing—first manifested in an amateur newspaper he produces with his younger brother.

1899:

Much encouraged by his mother-in-law ("Frank Baum, you're a fool if you don't write down those stories!"), Baum publishes *Mother Goose in Prose* in 1897 and achieves bestseller status two years later with a volume of jingles for children, *Father Goose: His Book* (above). Delightfully illustrated by William Wallace Denslow, the book establishes the Baum/Denslow team as a leading purveyor of juvenile fare.

JANUARY 20, 1903:

The Wizard of Oz opens on Broadway, an extravaganza prepared for the stage by Baum but vastly rewritten and reconfigured under the aegis of legendary director Julian Mitchell. Baum's intended pantomime for children becomes instead a melange of topical humor and vaudevillian performances, uproariously entertaining to both young and old; it's the season's biggest hit. Fred Stone and David Montgomery rise to instant fame as the Scarecrow and the Tin Woodman, and *Oz* plays 293 New York performances. Thereafter, road companies tour the show for the next six years.

1904:

Due to overwhelming demand from his young fans, Baum publishes the first *Oz* sequel: *The Marvelous Land of Oz*. Before his death 15 years later, Baum will go on to write a half-dozen Oz short stories and a dozen more full-length Oz novels. The latter include *Ozma of Oz* (1907), *Dorothy and the Wizard in Oz* (1908) (pictured above), *The Road to Oz* (1909), *The Emerald City of Oz* (1910), and—from 1913–1920—*The Patchwork Girl of Oz*, *Tik-Tok of Oz*, *The Scarecrow of Oz*, *Rinkitink in Oz*, *The Lost Princess of Oz*, *The Tin Woodman of Oz*, *The Magic of Oz*, and *Glinda of Oz*.

1910:

Baum and Maud move to Hollywood and build a home he christens "Ozcot." In addition to his Oz work, the author continues to pen other fantasy tales for children, novels for adults, and several series of books for teen readers. When not writing, he golfs and proudly tends his gardens (shown above), ultimately winning additional fame as a champion amateur horticulturist of Southern California.

AUGUST 6, 1914:

The Patchwork Girl of Oz, a silent-film adaptation of the 1913 *Oz* book is written and released by Baum himself as the first production of the Oz Film Company. The picture stars a teenage French acrobat, Pierre Couderc (pictured above), in the title role. Later that year, Baum produces *The Magic Cloak of Oz* and *His Majesty, the Scarecrow of Oz*, but his movies fail because of distribution problems and the lack of a ready audience for "family" film fare at that time.

MAY 6, 1919:

Just shy of his 63rd birthday, L. Frank Baum (pictured below) dies at Ozcot after years of tireless work but failing health. In the preceding 22 years, he has published over 60 books, written or produced nearly a score of musical scripts, prepared silent film scenarios, and left an inestimable legacy in his creation of the first American fairy tale and its environs and inhabitants. *The Wonderful Wizard of Oz* and its sequels prove timeless and cross-generational in their appeal.

1921:

Loath to see the end of such a successful series, Baum's publishers select Ruth Plumly Thompson as the next "Royal Historian of Oz." *The Royal Book of Oz* is the first of 19 annual Thompson Oz titles, and pictures for her books are contributed (as they have been to the Baum Oz books since 1904) by the incomparable John R. Neill. The illustrator himself writes three Oz titles in 1940–42; by 1963, when the series officially concludes, there are 40 Oz books in all.

JANUARY 5, 1975:

The Wiz, a rock musical version of the first Oz book with an all-black cast, opens on Broadway at the Majestic Theatre. With songs by Charlie Smalls and a book by William F. Brown, the production wins five Tony Awards and runs for 1,672 performances. Conceptually, *The Wiz* is a gamble that pays off: The story is drawn from Baum's book rather than the MGM film, and its combination of soul, humor, and scorching performances captivates both standard theatergoers and a new African-American audience. A film version, starring Diana Ross and Michael Jackson, is produced in 1978.

JUNE 21, 1985:

Disney releases *Return to Oz*, a $30 million live-action motion picture written and directed by renowned editor and cameraman Walter Murch.

OCTOBER 1973:

Elton John's *Goodbye Yellow Brick Road* is released and spends 84 weeks on the UK album chart and 103 weeks on the US album chart, hitting number one on both. The title song by John (pictured above) and Bernie Taupin contains a wistful lyric, reminiscent of Dorothy and the cyclone: "When are you gonna come down/When are you going to land/I should have stayed on the farm/I should have listened to my old man."

SEPTEMBER 1995:

Wicked: The Life and Times of the Wicked Witch of the West, a novel by Gregory Maguire, is published by ReganBooks. He begins with the premise that the cackling, broom-riding, green-skinned Wicked Witch of the West may not have started out evil. In a rich, literary style that recalls J. R. R. Tolkien and Angela Carter, Maguire creates an alternative Oz in which the Wizard is a sinister fascist figure and the Witch (whom he names Elphaba) is a freedom fighter for the rights of talking Animals.

AUGUST 15, 1939:

The Grauman's Chinese Theatre premieres Metro-Goldwyn-Mayer's *The Wizard of Oz*. An immediate critical and popular triumph, the now-legendary movie musical stars Judy Garland as Dorothy. The following year, it receives five Academy Award nominations (including Best Picture) and wins Oscars for Best Music/Original Score and Best Song ("Over the Rainbow"). Garland is presented with a juvenile Oscar for her "outstanding contributions to the screen" by frequent costar Mickey Rooney, pictured here below.

NOVEMBER 3, 1956:

MGM's *Oz* launches what will become an unprecedented career as a television mainstay. The premiere telecast draws 53 percent of that night's viewing audience. By the time the film's virtually annual appearance leaves the networks and goes to cable in 1999, there is no way to calculate the billions who have embraced the movie as an icon of childhood and entertainment. The initial showing is cohosted by "Cowardly Lion" Bert Lahr and Judy Garland's ten-year-old daughter, Liza Minnelli (shown here, left, at a special preview screening with her three-year-old half-sister Lorna Luft).

JANUARY 1, 1957:

Sixteen fans of the Oz series form The International Wizard of Oz Club, with its avowed mission to bring together those interested in L. Frank Baum and Oz. Today, the club counts its worldwide membership in the thousands and publishes a trimonthly magazine, *The Baum Bugle*, which features popular and scholarly articles about Oz, its creators, dramatizations, and collectibles. The club also holds annual conventions at different locations around the United States each year, where members screen rare film and television footage, present lectures, and exhibit Ozian artifacts.

MAY 24, 2000:

A pair of Dorothy's ruby-red slippers from MGM's *The Wizard of Oz* is auctioned at Christie's East in New York for $666,000. Movie memorabilia collector David Elkouby purchases the red-sequined size 6B shoes—which may have been used for dancing scenes in the movie. They were previously owned by Anthony Landini, who bought them at a 1988 Christie's auction for $165,000. But the first owner of the slippers was Roberta Bauman, who won them in a 1940 movie-trivia contest and kept them for 48 years.

JUNE 22, 2004:

"Over the Rainbow" is ranked the "number one" motion picture song of all time in a poll conducted by The American Film Institute; coincidentally, the announcement comes on the 35th anniversary of Judy Garland's passing.

MARCH 7, 2005:

Wicked kicks off a national tour with a seven-week engagement in Toronto at the Canon Theatre. The tour will visit more than 80 cities.

OCTOBER 30, 2003:

Wicked, a musical based on Gregory Maguire's novel, opens at the Gershwin Theatre on Broadway. Richard Zoglin of *Time* magazine writes: "*Wicked* works because it has something Broadway musicals, so addicted to facetiousness and camp, have largely given up on: a story that adults can take seriously . . . . If every musical had a brain, a heart, and the courage of *Wicked*, Broadway really would be a magical place."

DECEMBER 9, 2004:

The original Broadway cast recording of Stephen Schwartz's *Wicked* is among the top album sellers on Broadway. Popular on iPods and computers, *Wicked* also ranks among iTunes's "2004 Top 10 Soundtrack Albums." Titles listed as the "Top Downloads" from the album include "Defying Gravity," "Popular," "For Good," and "What Is This Feeling?"

JUNE 24, 2005:

Wicked opens its third company at the Ford Center for the Performing Arts—the same theater (then known as the Oriental Theatre) where Baby Frances Gumm sang in 1934, and emcee George Jessup changed her last name to Garland. She chose "Judy" for herself a year later.

JUNE 6, 2004:

At the 2004 Tony Awards, *Wicked* is represented by winners Idina Menzel (pictured below with producer David Stone) for Best Actress in a Musical, Eugene Lee for Best Scenic Design, and Susan Hilferty for Best Costume Design.

DECEMBER 21, 2004:

The producers of *Wicked* announce that the musical has recouped its $14 million investment 14 months after opening. Whereas it takes even successful shows two or three years to earn back their investment—and about 80 percent never do—*Wicked* is doing $1.2 million per week in box office and playing to soldout houses.

FEBRUARY 13, 2005:

Composer-lyricist Stephen Schwartz wins the Grammy Award for Best Musical Show Album.

OCTOBER 30, 2005:

Wicked celebrates the second anniversary of its Broadway opening.

ARE PEOPLE BORN

WICKED?

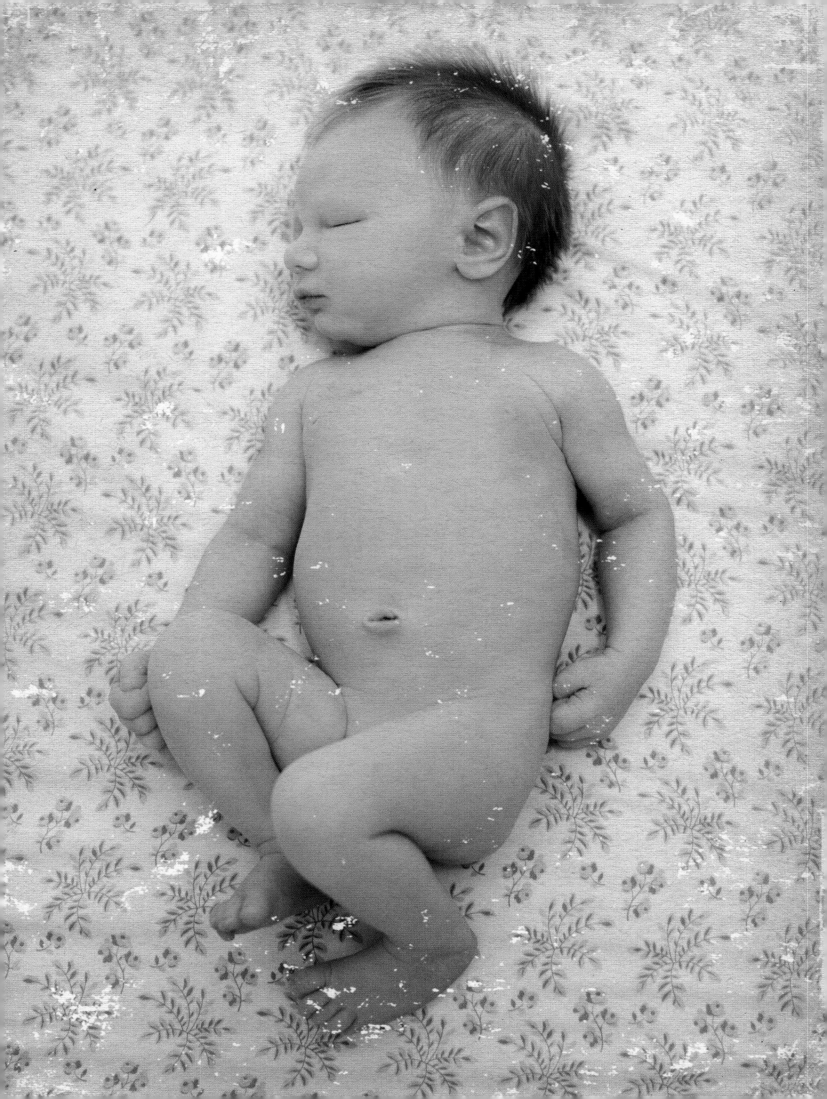

PLATE I.

NO GOOD DEED GOES UNPUNISHED / NO ACT OF CHARITY GOES UNRESENTED

CHAPTER I

WHAT IS THIS FEELING?

IN THE FALL OF 2003, IT WAS EASY TO BE A JADED LOVER OF Broadway. The Great White Way was doing brisk business—box office was up $50 million from the previous year—and most shows had rebounded from the economy-depressing attacks of September 11, 2001. Artistically speaking, the dominant feeling was one of savvy commercialism coupled with a wry disenchantment with the power of musicals to lift the spirit. Shows such as *The Producers*, *Urinetown*, and *Hairspray* proved there was a mood of irreverent spoofing. These hits excelled at parody and pastiche par excellence, satirizing the conventions and tunes of traditional musicals. *The Producers*' plot hinged on a turkey of a show being mistaken as brilliant; *Urinetown* mocked audience expectations for a happy ending. Individually, the productions were clever and entertaining, but Broadway aficionados worried that the musical would never be taken seriously again.

Another trend on Broadway was the "jukebox musical," which recycled familiar songbooks. This new hybrid had its hits: *Mamma Mia!* and *Movin' Out* set the tunes of ABBA and

Billy Joel, respectively, to rather thin stories. But for fans who hungered for original scores from seasoned songwriters—the new sound of the 21st century—there was a nagging sense of déjà vu about these projects.

This was the milieu that *Wicked* entered on October 8th, when its previews began at the Gershwin Theatre. Critics were wary of the premise, a girl-power gloss on *The Wizard of Oz*, with sumptuous sets, elaborate special effects, and power ballads. It sounded like a throwback to the 1980s, when treacly spectacles like *The Phantom of the Opera* and *Cats* tried to win hearts with flashy sets and bombastic emotions. From another angle, the concept sounded potentially precious and narrow in its appeal. Certainly, everyone loves *The Wizard of Oz*, but not everyone wants a new take on it. Not all theater critics were familiar with the book the show was based on, Gregory Maguire's *Wicked: The Life and Times of the Wicked Witch of the West*. This witty, engrossing fantasy upset ideas about the world created by L. Frank Baum in 1900. In its sensibility and moral seriousness, the book—an untold history of the Wicked Witch—was both playful and firmly intellectual.

Although the source material was potentially rich, there have been few successful twists on *The Wizard of Oz*: There was a 1985 movie sequel, a stage and film version of *The Wiz*, and several cartoon versions of the story. All helped to keep Baum's Oz firmly lodged in the cultural unconscious of Americans, but, as with all cultural icons, they also had the effect of diluting its power. When the Wicked Witch of the West flies across a schoolgirl's lunchbox or comes knocking on Halloween, her status as the incarnation of evil tends to diminish.

And yet *Wicked*, the Broadway musical, swept these doubts away like, yes, a Kansas cyclone. Entering the Gershwin Theatre, the audience was immediately struck by the set: The pre-show curtain was a massive map of Oz as they had never seen it, ringed by a set that seemed built of massive clockwork cogs intertwined with barren vines. Perched atop the proscenium was the imposing Clock of the Time Dragon, a giant metallic puppet with hinged jaws and scary wings. Fans of the novel would immediately recognize this ominous contraption from the novel (see CHAPTER 2: WONDERFUL for more details on the adaptation), but everyone else could simply enjoy it as part of the exquisite design's overall phantasmagoria. Those who thought they'd seen it all on Broadway had one definite thought: Toto, I don't think we're in Kansas anymore.

As *Wicked* unfolded, the wonder and excitement grew. Book writer Winnie Holzman had evoked the fantasy world of Oz without spoofing the source. The jokes landed, the plot moved. And Stephen Schwartz's score covered an amazing amount of stylistic ground: haunting medieval-style choruses, up-tempo comic numbers, pop, and classical-flavored anthems. Then there were killer numbers, such as "Defying Gravity," a soaring song of self-empowerment with emotional thrills and eye-popping special effects that moved spectators to cheers.

Wicked quickly took on a life of its own, generating fantastic word of mouth and astonishing box-office returns. Records were broken, awards were given, and fans returned multiple times. But more on that later. First, we'll look behind the scenes and into the minds of the people who created *Wicked*.

Part One

IN THE BEGINNING

 REGORY MAGUIRE ALWAYS HAD PROBLEMS WITH *THE WIZARD OF OZ.* WHILE MOST CHILDREN JOYFULLY (AND UNQUESTIONINGLY) FOLLOWED THE ADVENTURES OF DOROTHY, TOTO, AND THEIR PECULIAR STRAW, TIN, AND LEONINE PROTECTORS THROUGH THE MAGICAL REALM OF OZ,

the future novelist dwelled on the tale's moral implications. Why did the Wizard command Dorothy to kill the Wicked Witch? Merely because she was wicked, with a capital W? Why did Glinda the Good Witch wait until Dorothy had nearly been killed to tell her that the shoes would take her home to Kansas? By age 39, Maguire—then a successful author of a dozen children's novels— knew that the time had come to pen a book that explored the darker corners of Oz, to find out if that infamous black-clad crone on the broomstick was actually misunderstood.

Soon after his adult-oriented "prequel" hit the shelves to mostly positive reviews and a soon-to-be-cult readership, movie offers came pouring in. Marc Platt, a producer at Universal, saw a golden opportunity for a new film, if only a screenplay could be crafted from the book. Winnie Holzman, the celebrated TV scriptwriter (*thirtysomething*, *My So-Called Life*) had discovered the strange and provocative volume in a New York bookshop, and her imagination started churning. The third major player in this story of origins—and the one who made all the difference—was a composer-lyricist who hadn't had a hit on Broadway for about three decades. Stephen Schwartz had already secured his place in Broadway history books

for *Godspell* (1971), *Pippin* (1972), and *The Magic Show* (1974). His efforts had netted him a handful of Tony Award nominations, but in recent years he had turned his songwriting talents to Hollywood projects, such as the award-winning scores for a series of animated films: *Pocahontas* (1995), *The Hunchback of Notre Dame* (1996), and *The Prince of Egypt* (1999). These are the disparate artists, separated by media and geography, who would eventually come to one realization: This book would make a great show.

GREGORY MAGUIRE (*Novelist*): I first got the notion for *Wicked* in 1988, as a novel for adults, but at the time, I didn't think I was a skilled enough writer. Then in 1990, I moved to London with my then-boyfriend when the first Gulf War started. I found myself riveted by how the British press vilified Saddam Hussein to galvanize public opinion in support of the military action against Iraq. I mean, I agreed that Saddam Hussein was a villain, but my politics were less important than my noticing how the British press used certain words to draw attention to the need for military intervention. I came back from London at Easter time and found that, without my quite having noticed it, my politics had shifted way to the right. And I took myself

---

THE NOVEL THAT STARTED IT ALL

Wicked: The Life and Times of the Wicked Witch of the West, *by Gregory Maguire (ReganBooks, 1995)*

to task for it: "Wait a minute. You're a progressive liberal. How did this happen? How did you lose your moorings so quickly?" That's when I realized that I could marry these concerns to questions I had when I first thought of the idea of *Wicked*: Was it possible for someone to change his moral stripe? To be born blameless and become evil? Or does one have kind of a kernel of evil inside, like cells that are predisposed to be cancerous? At that point, the project took shape. So the idea was to write the story of someone who really was bad. But the minute that Elphaba appeared on the page—sharp-toothed, smelling like dog urine, appearing more of a beast than a human being—I couldn't help but love her as a parent loves a child. I couldn't make her as bad as I originally thought she was going to be. But I couldn't make her a saint, either. She's a little bit morally corrupt in the novel. And toward the end, when Dorothy lands in Oz, the Witch is having sleeping problems. Anyone who has suffered any kind of serious insomnia, even for 24 hours, knows that you lose your way very quickly. So her being hysterical in the last 40 or 50 pages of the novel is directly related to panic and sleep deprivation. She's having a nervous breakdown. Is that the same thing as being bad? Anyway, the book was published in 1995. There was a rather dismissive review by the *New York Times*, which was regrettable, but it didn't keep the book from becoming an early favorite of readers, including one critic for the *Los Angeles Times* who gave it a front-page review. The following week, I began to get movie offers. Whoopi Goldberg was curious. But it was Demi Moore and her then–production company who put an option on it with Universal. Whether Moore was going to be in it or not, I don't know, but they worked on developing a screenplay for about three years.

MARC PLATT (*Producer*): When I became president of production at Universal, the book was here. Demi Moore's production company had optioned *Wicked*, and it was one of the projects I targeted as a great idea for a

film, because I loved it so much. But, despite our best effort, we felt the screenplay was actually not quite working. It lacked something; it wasn't quite magical.

STEPHEN SCHWARTZ (*Composer-lyricist*): I was in Hawaii on a snorkeling trip with friends of mine in December 1996. My best friend is a songwriter named John Bucchino. I had been visiting him, and we went snorkeling with the singer Holly Near. On the boat back, Holly said, "You know, I'm reading this really interesting book. It's *The Wizard of Oz* story from the Wicked Witch of the West's point of view." I was intrigued immediately. It sounded so much like my kind of material. So when I got back to the mainland the following day, I started to read the book and was only a little ways into it, and I had my lawyer find out where the rights lay: Demi Moore's production company and, ultimately, Marc Platt at Universal.

MARC PLATT: The screenplay was kind of dense, and I kept wanting to go deeper into the story of the relationship between Galinda and Elphaba. What are these two women doing in the same frame? The screenplay didn't quite get at that. It stuck more closely to Gregory's novel. In order to get at that kind of story, we needed inner dialogue, which is very hard to accomplish cinematically.

WINNIE HOLZMAN (*Book writer*): In 1996, I was in a bookstore in New York—in one of those bookstore dazes—and I saw *Wicked*, the paperback, with that incredible cover of a green girl with her face hidden by the black hat. And it really affected me. I had this feeling like, "Oh my God this is such a brilliant idea." As soon as I read the back of the book, I understood the premise. So I bought it, but I didn't read it. I called my agent and I said, "How do I get the rights to this?" At that point, I was thinking only of trying to write it as a movie. And she immediately came back to me:

MARC PLATT

"Universal has the rights to it. They already started on the screenplay." So I put the book on the shelf in my workroom, in a very prominent place because I liked the cover so well. But I didn't even read the book, because I was bummed that I wasn't going to be working on it.

STEPHEN SCHWARTZ: After several months, I met with Marc in 1997 and basically tried to talk him out of doing *Wicked* as a movie. I believe they were awaiting their second draft of the screenplay. That's how far they'd gotten. I told him that I felt it had to be a musical and more specifically begin life onstage. I was lucky that Marc had a background in musical theater. My plea was not falling on entirely deaf ears.

WINNIE HOLZMAN: Stephen and I were having lunch, and he said "Well, you know, it should be a musical for Broadway." And my jaw dropped open. And I was like "Oh my God, he's right." But then we were just sort of looking at each other shrugging, going isn't it sad that they're planning a movie. I just thought he was so smart to think of that—to think of making it a musical, which had never occurred to me. But that's why he's him.

MARC PLATT: Stephen asked, "Have you ever thought about turning this into a musical?" And a light bulb went on, and I thought, "This is exactly what is missing from the screenplay." First, we all think of Oz as a musical world: For many of us, the main reference point is the 1939 film. Second, music lends itself to the heightened nature of a fantasy world. Third, in a musical, a character can literally turn to the audience and sing about what he or she is feeling.

STEPHEN SCHWARTZ: There was a period of time when Marc was developing

Wicked on two tracks: as a nonmusical film and as a stage musical. Eventually, the stage musical took over. But it took about a year for the decision to be made: Yes, we're going to go ahead and do this.

MARC PLATT: For a book writer, Stephen suggested Winnie Holzman. Winnie I had known from television. Again, I was interested in telling the story of the girls. And my favorite work of Winnie's is the show she created, *My So-Called Life*. If you think about that show and the angst of the Claire Danes character, it felt like a good marriage of writer to play.

WINNIE HOLZMAN: The second Stephen started to talk to me about doing *Wicked* with him, my overwhelming feeling was, I'm going to learn so much.

GREGORY MAGUIRE: In November 1998, I got a phone call from Stephen Schwartz's lawyers, and I agreed to meet Stephen. He drove up from his Connecticut home and we went for a walk in the woods, around my then-boyfriend's—now husband's—family farm. He talked as if I might have an antipathy for musicals, but I've always loved the musical theater. I even had hopes as a teenager to go into it. But I have a poker face, a Scottish Calvinist sort of demeanor, when I need to. So

STEPHEN SCHWARTZ AND GREGORY MAGUIRE

I just listened. And he was very persuasive. I knew his work well: *Pippin* and *Godspell*. I had played songs from *Godspell* in my Catholic Church when I was a choir director. So Stephen was very much a celebrity in my mind. He said, "You've written a story with a lot of strong emotion, and it can stand being sung directly to an audience." Then he described how the play might open, with the first couple of lines of lyrics from "No One Mourns the Wicked." And he had me right there. However seriocomic *Wicked* might become eventually, or however the story might be changed, as long as the fundamental questions about behavior, appearance, deception, honesty, and courage were represented, then I was happy. And I could say *yes*.

Part Two

EARLY WORKSHOPS

 OW BEGAN THE LONG, TORTUOUS PROCESS OF TURNING A 400-PAGE NOVEL FULL OF INCIDENT, CHARACTER, AND DETAIL INTO A SHOW. SCHWARTZ AND HOLZMAN, WITH FEEDBACK FROM PLATT, BRAINSTORMED, WROTE, REWROTE, AND REVISED AGAIN. READINGS WERE HELD and songs were performed for select audience members. Before Idina Menzel was cast as Elphaba, L.A. actress Stephanie J. Block read and sang the part in rehearsals. (She would go on to play the part in the first national tour of *Wicked*.) Kristin Chenoweth, a 1999 Tony Award–winner for *You're a Good Man, Charlie Brown* and one of the hottest young talents to hit Broadway in years, joined the process in September 2000. Throughout about two years of intensive work, the creative team conducted seven crucial readings in Los Angeles and New York as the book and score evolved bit by bit.

MARC PLATT: In our first year working together, Stephen, Winnie, and I sat in my office, and we literally beat for beat worked out the story to *Wicked*. I work on index cards and put them on a bulletin board. I still have my stack of file cards, which altered over time, but nobody went off to work—though Stephen had a song or two—until we had literally beat out the show scene by scene, character by character, until we thought we had a beginning, middle, and end. It wasn't until those note cards were finished that Stephen went off to do the music and Winnie went off to write the first draft of the book.

STEPHEN SCHWARTZ: The very first reading was out in Los Angeles in the spring of 2000. We read the first act at the Coronet Theater. It was a table reading, basically. The first act, at that point, was over two hours long. Shows tend to start out longer and then one finds what one can cull. That was just for a few people. We learned quite a good deal from that.

WINNIE HOLZMAN: I knew I wanted the story to have a love triangle between these two women and Fiyero. Obviously, there are seeds of that in the novel. Stephen loved that right away. In September of 2000, Marc got us a big room at Universal for, like, two weeks, and we rehearsed what we had. We put together our second big reading to hear it out loud; it was still very

{OPPOSITE, TOP} *Marc Platt, Stephen Schwartz, and Winnie Holzman hammered out an early version of the* Wicked *plot in Platt's office on countless index cards. Some ideas made it into the final version, such as "College—Meet: Morrible—Teaches sorcery—only to select few" (second card from right) whereas others didn't quite, such as "CRYSTAL BALL—Cornfields—Tries spell to save F[iyero]" (second from left).*

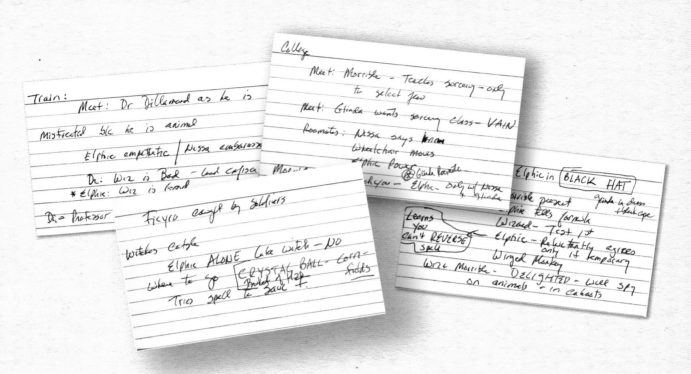

long then and the plot was pretty confusing. But we had Kristin for the first time. It changed the whole plot. Suddenly, it was all about the friendship between Glinda and Elphaba.

STEPHEN SCHWARTZ: I knew that Kristin was in Los Angeles at the time, and called her and asked her to do it. I had thought immediately of Kristin to read the part of Glinda. Of course, I knew her work from the Broadway shows *Steel Pier* and *You're A Good Man, Charlie Brown*. Fortunately, she liked the material and thought it would be good for her. And we just knew that she was perfect for the role. From that point on, she was in.

KRISTIN CHENOWETH (*Original Glinda*): In 2000, I was out in L.A. doing my sitcom, *Kristin*, for NBC. Stephen Schwartz called and said he had a project that he was writing with me in mind, and could I do the reading? You know, at that point I was so tired, and really reluctant. But then I read it, and thought, "I definitely want to do this reading." So I did.

STEPHANIE J. BLOCK (*Elphaba in development workshops and* Wicked *national tour*): Stephen wasn't too familiar with the musical theater actors out in L.A., and I was recommended to him, back in February of 2000. We started out presenting Universal Pictures with three songs. Then a reading of Act I, which at that point was over two hours long, so they did a cut. I did a lot of the readings and presentations for two years out in Los Angeles and it was a fascinat-

{BOTTOM} KRISTIN CHENOWETH, WINNIE HOLZMAN, AND IDINA MENZEL

ing process. I was a lover of *The Wizard of Oz*, so it intrigued me to find this entire story from the perspectives of Glinda and Elphaba.

KRISTIN CHENOWETH: I just was in there doing my thing! I think what happened is that people started seeing the chemistry between me and Stephanie and thinking, "Oh, my God: This might be about Elphaba and Glinda, not just Elphaba." The next thing I know, the show is about two witches. It just grew into that. I don't think it was an accident. When I first started, Glinda was very much a supporting character. And then it just kind of grew into the part that it became. But in that early three-hour Act I reading, Glinda was hardly in it.

STEPHANIE J. BLOCK: Stephen's songs touched me right away: the earliest ones I heard were "Making Good," which has since been replaced with "The Wizard and I," "One Short Day," and "As Long As You're Mine." Each of those songs had such a completely different feel to them. And I was familiar with Stephen's music in *Godspell*, so I knew it was something special before I had even read a line or seen a costume or knew the concept of the piece.

STEPHEN SCHWARTZ: We rewrote the first act and did a draft of the second act. Then we did a couple of readings at Universal pretty close together in February and March of 2001, with some work in between. Then we would go back and forth basically between readings that were done on the Universal movie lot and a couple that were done in rehearsal studios in New York.

MARC PLATT: One of the most memorable moments of our journey occurred at Universal in March of 2001 when we held the first reading of the entire book and score. Although Stephen, Winnie, and I knew that *Wicked* was very entertaining and satisfying, none of us were prepared for the overwhelming emotional response generated by that reading. Every single person in that room was moved beyond words, including the three of us. As the last note concluded, the room burst into thunderous and sustained applause and Winnie, Stephen, and I looked at each other. We knew at that moment we were ready to move on.

SUDDENLY, IT WAS ALL ABOUT THE FRIENDSHIP BETWEEN GLINDA AND ELPHABA.

—WINNIE HOLZMAN

Part Three

ENTER A DIRECTOR

 Y THE TIME JOE MANTELLO JOINED THE CREATIVE TEAM AS DIRECTOR, HE WAS ALREADY AN ESTABLISHED FORCE IN THEATER—JUST NOT MUSICAL THEATER. MANTELLO STARTED AS A DRAMATIC ACTOR, MOST NOTABLY AS LOUIS IRONSON IN TONY KUSHNER'S LEGENDARY EPIC *ANGELS IN AMERICA*

in 1994. Since then, he had gone on to stage critically acclaimed plays, such as Terrence McNally's *Love! Valour! Compassion!* and the Tony Award–winning baseball drama *Take Me Out*. In the summer of 2001, when he joined *Wicked*, no one considered Mantello a director of big-scale musicals. True, he had directed a new opera, *Dead Man Walking*, for the San Francisco Opera, and was developing a chamber musical, A *Man of No Importance*, for Lincoln Center Theater, but even he admitted that a project such as *Wicked* was of a different scale entirely. Nevertheless, Mantello's skill at crafting drama was essential: With him at the helm, development of the story accelerated; he helped detect which plotlines were interesting and which were dragging the show down. Mantello also presided over the New York auditions for *Wicked*'s Elphaba (Kristin Chenoweth was already selected to play Glinda on Broadway), in which a young, rising star named Idina Menzel made quite an impression.

MARC PLATT: As we prepared to move forward, it was important to me to bring on a producing partner who not only had the management, production, and

marketing experience to produce a large Broadway musical, but shared my passion for the project. I had been introduced several years earlier to David Stone, who, as a successful producer, had precisely such experience. David attended the reading in March of 2001 at Universal, and as I happened to glance at him during the performance of "For Good," I saw tears streaming down his face. It was then that I knew I'd found the right man.

DAVID STONE (*Producer*): Joe and I had worked together several times before. I told Marc, Stephen, and Winnie that Joe would be ideal because he is both a writer's director and a painter, in a way. Because he had done so many new plays, he knows how to help writers refine and restructure their vision. And, he has this amazing visual imagination. *Wicked*, with its intricate plot and its other-worldly physical manifestation, needed someone with his skills. I gave him the script on a Friday night and he called Saturday morning at nine o'clock, which was strange; Joe doesn't usually wake up that early on a weekend. Apparently, he was pumped, and had been waiting till the clock struck nine before he called me. And he said, "Okay, this is what works. And this is what needs to be fixed." He had all these ideas.

{OPPOSITE} KRISTIN CHENOWETH (GLINDA) AND STEPHANIE J. BLOCK (ELPHABA)

{ABOVE} JOE MANTELLO

He understood the very tricky tone so completely upon first reading the script. I called Marc and Stephen and told them, "You know, this could be very exciting."

JOE MANTELLO (*Director*): The most obvious difference between directing plays and musicals is the nature of the collaboration. In working on a play, there's something manageable about the director-playwright relationship. It's very intimate, and I've been fortunate to work with playwrights who were completely in sync. In a musical, more people get to vote. So it's a bit trickier to navigate. But alternately, the good thing is, if there are enough smart people in the room, problem solving becomes more exciting. I received the script, along with a CD that came out of that second reading of the entire show in March 2001. The show started very, very differently, with people walking up and down the aisles of the theater hawking souvenirs from the Cowardly Lion and the Tin Woodman. I mean, it began after the witch's death, but it was more satirical. The very first person you saw was Madame Morrible, announcing that the Wicked Witch was dead. She then brought out Dorothy, the Lion, the Scarecrow, and the Tin Woodman. And the Scarecrow sang "No One Mourns the Wicked." Initially, I was concerned about seeing those four iconic characters right off the bat. It might be jarring to an audience. And, in fact, I wondered if they should be seen at all. I mean, obvi-

ously the Scarecrow and the Tin Woodman needed to be seen, but I wondered if the Lion and Dorothy should ever be seen, because they're so etched in our psyches. And I just felt like beginning with them wasn't the best idea. At that point, Kristin had done all the readings. And it was maybe another draft before we realized that it should be Glinda who started the show, floating down in her bubble machine.

KRISTIN CHENOWETH: Joe really appreciates an actor that brings a lot to the table. And I'm willing to do anything to get to the place I need to be. Between the fearlessness that I had, and the fearlessness he had about the piece, we really hit it off. He had some great ideas that were implemented and became integral to the show. Even how the set looked, and how our costumes looked. I loved the fact that he cared so much, right down to the hat you wore. And a lot of directors are like, "Whatever. You have the basic gist of it, so let's go." But Joe really cared. I mean, he cared so much about the length of my hair! I wasn't sure if he wanted to be me, or what. And we talked and wrestled and finally found the length that we both agreed would fit with Glinda.

JOE MANTELLO: I loved Idina in *Rent*. She was actually the first person who came into the room to audition for the show in New York. It was about a week and a half after September 11th, so we were all really still kind of shaky. But we had to keep moving forward because we had this workshop coming up in December. And Idina embraced the green early on.

IDINA MENZEL (*Original Elphaba*): I guess it was kind of crazy, but I just wanted to give a nod to the character for the audition, so I wore green eye shadow and some green lipstick and made myself look kind of dreary: smoky black eyes, dark, ratty clothes, to feel a little grungy. That's how I saw Elphaba after I read the novel.

JOE MANTELLO: She even had green blush on her face! I don't know where you find that kind of make-up…. She was the first person to walk in the room, and we all loved her. I remember Winnie in particular—who didn't know her—was really taken. And then when

IDINA MENZEL

Idina came back for the second audition, I think that's when it became really clear to us that she was the perfect choice. I mean, she hit "Defying Gravity" out of the ballpark, though while she was singing it, she got to the end where she goes, "Never gonna bring me—" and her voice cracked really badly. I think she swore! And then hit the final note. And she went home crying because she thought she screwed it up.

IDINA MENZEL: You often tell yourself, "Oh, I don't care if I get this," so you won't get your hopes up. But I just felt a connection to the character and the whole project. I felt like I really needed to be doing it, and I knew that I would kill to work with Joe Mantello and Stephen Schwartz. That I would just have this amazing experience and grow as an artist. But I did kind of screw up the song. I didn't hit the high note as well as I should have, and actually swore in the middle of the song because I cracked. I thought, "Either they'll love it and think, 'Boy, that's one good witch there.'" Or they'll think I was completely inappropriate. So I left kicking myself. And yet, something in me knew that I had the essence of this character and I believed they would see that.

JOE MANTELLO: Ultimately, it sort of made her more endearing. Idina is so original and so ethereal, kind of a mess in such a great way. It makes her the perfect counterpoint with how solid Kristin is. They had incredible chemistry from the first day until the day that Kristin left the show. Their onstage chemistry was remarkable. And even though offstage they are very different people, when they got together, to me it was magical.

STEPHEN SCHWARTZ: Idina gives the impression of being very "downtown," as if she shows up without any preparation and just operates on instinct. That's part of her persona, but that's not who she is. She worked with a vocal coach very hard and specifically for months on the score. Oddly enough, the high notes were not a problem for her. Some were even determined by her. She took things up above where they were written, and I'd say, "That's great, do that." What she worked on was her mid-range and the warmth of the low range in songs like "For Good" and "I'm Not That Girl." She also worked on having an effortless run from the very low part of her range up through the high part. Idina has that really strong high vocal, and she always had a sort of breathy Cyndi Lauper–like low voice. But what she worked on strengthening was the mid-range. And she worked very, very hard.

IDINA MENZEL: We did about a year and a half of readings and workshops. The writers would work on the material and we'd put it up in front of the producers and industry people to get feedback. Then Stephen and Winnie might take two months to rewrite a song and work on scenes. Then we'd fly out to L.A. and do it again for Universal. It's an amazing process to be part of. The more the writers get to know you, the more they start to write musically for you. They'd be inspired by Kristin and me— by our personas—and infuse them into the characters. And then, finally, we had to actually put the show on its feet, instead of singing in front of music stands and doing it in a fluorescent-lit rehearsal room. And so we finally got to San Francisco. You know, for out-of-town tryouts, sometimes the producers don't put it up in its complete form. That's to save money and just see how audiences respond to the show. But with Marc and David, they wanted to really figure out what this land of Oz was going to look like; they had to build what we were going to do for Broadway and take a risk on this world.

Kristin Chenoweth and Idina Menzel in rehearsal, San Francisco, May 2003

Part Four

ON THE ROAD:
SAN FRANCISCO

HE OUT-OF-TOWN TRYOUT IS A TIME-HONORED RITUAL FOR THE BROADWAY MUSICAL. IN THE TRYOUTS, A SHOW'S CREATIVE TEAM CAN TEST THE PRODUCT OUT ON AUDIENCES AND GET A FEEL FOR WHAT WORKS AND WHAT DOESN'T. TRYOUTS CAN BE EXHAUSTING BUT VALUABLE PERIODS in which the team fine-tunes a hit. Shows can literally be saved out of town, as the book writer feverishly tweaks scenes that don't work or gags that fall flat. The composer, meanwhile, might find inspiration and pen a new song that goes on to be a show's big hit. By May 28, 2003, when the curtain rose on *Wicked*'s first preview for a paying audience at the Curran Theatre in San Francisco, the period in which we could learn from mistakes we had made or discover things that didn't work as well as we thought they did—as well as things that worked better than we thought they would. In retrospect, it was the right thing to do. The other strategic move we made was to decide way ahead of time that regardless of what happened in San Francisco, we were going to shut the production down for a few months before we were

TO AN OUTSIDE EYE, THE TWEAKS WE MADE
IN SAN FRANCISCO PROBABLY LOOK MINOR.
TO US, THEY WERE ENORMOUS.

—JOE MANTELLO

material had been in development for about three-and-a-half years. The script had gone through countless permutations; songs had been written, rewritten, and scrapped. Whole story lines had been built up and others trimmed back. And the work still wasn't done.

MARC PLATT: It was more expensive and more risky, but we decided to go with a first-class production for San Francisco tryouts. We found that not only did the city embrace the show, but it was a very constructive

going to New York. The decision was made long before we ever opened in San Francisco. We wanted to ensure that the time was there to make crucial changes that might be needed—in the book or the score or elements of the design. It turned out that we used every minute of that down time to make improvements.

DAVID STONE: It is always a great opportunity for a new show to try out far away from New York. Broadway audiences are perhaps a bit judgemental. They expect a finished product. San Francisco allowed us to make mistakes and learn. And, because people were away from their day-to-day lives, the entire company and creative team were together constantly. So, everyone works more intensely—and gets the chance to really bond.

WINNIE HOLZMAN: It's funny. When I look back at San Francisco, I feel like it was so blessed. But at the time, I felt, you know, very lonely. I was away from my family in a hotel room, rewriting the show constantly. In a way, that single-mindedness is important. That's what it is to write a musical: You have to watch it over and over and respond to what you are seeing, and what the audience is seeing. You're dealing with a lot of different elements. Let's say the audience seems bored, or they don't seem interested in a certain song. Then you have to start asking questions, you know. "Is it the number itself? Is it the lighting? Is there something about the scene leading up to it that didn't set the number up properly?"

JOE MANTELLO: To an outside eye, the tweaks we made in San Francisco probably look minor. To us, they were enormous. There was so much plot that we had to set in motion so the story would pay off in Act II. The whole section at Shiz University was really complicated. We had to get several story lines in motion and give them their due without boring the audience. In an earlier version, we discovered near the end of Act I that Dr. Dillamond was dead. There was a funeral scene, where Galinda changed her name in front of all the mourners to Glinda. That was completely rewritten. We also had to give Elphaba a sense of humor. She was pretty earnest in San Francisco. And though people loved her, they were more delighted by Glinda because of her humor. So we tried to inject a little bit more fire and irony into Elphaba.

WINNIE HOLZMAN: You have to be very much like a detective with your fellow co-creators. It's almost a scientific process. But as soon as the audience comes in, it's an amazing experience. I mean, those first audiences were really into the show, even when it had awkward stretches and was too long. What got me through the whole San Francisco experience was Stephen, because he always made me laugh and we got along so well. And because he'd been through it so many times.

IDINA MENZEL: I stayed in the hotel literally next door to the Curran Theatre, so I didn't see anything of San Francisco. I was so committed to figuring out the part, and I was working really hard. The lines were changing every day. I was just struggling to figure Elphaba out, and we were trying to make the writing really strong for her. There's also the fact that you have to keep your voice in shape and stay healthy while doing eight shows a week. Everyone was saying, "Oh, you're working in San Francisco!" And I'm like, "Yeah, I watch movies in my hotel room and then crawl over to the theater and then crawl back to bed."

WINNIE HOLZMAN: Also, my hotel had a minibar. You have to understand that for someone like me, under pressure, this was a huge problem. And I didn't have the willpower to ask the hotel people to dismantle my minibar. So I was doing a lot of chocolate. Meanwhile, everyone around me was losing weight. Stephen in particular was driving me crazy because he was getting more and more fit. He was constantly playing tennis and swimming. David Stone and Marc Platt would "forget" to eat. And Joe just photosynthesizes. So there I was, running over to Macy's, because I was outgrowing all my clothes. And I would run into Kristin there, because she's a shopaholic like me. We were working in the same theater, staying in the same hotel, but I would only see Kristin at Macy's.

KRISTIN CHENOWETH: When Winnie or I needed to get away, or just be alone, we would find each other at Macy's. To me, Winnie was the real star of the show, because she really made the story work. If you read the novel, it is very different. And Winnie made that story stand out, to the point that audiences were moved eight times a week. I don't know if she will ever do another Broadway show, because it is not for wimps. But man, I hope she does, because she is so talented and so funny. She found my voice and all of the characters' voices. Besides that, she has really good taste in shopping. So there is a lot to love about her.

STEPHEN SCHWARTZ: The first preview, even if I've seen a model of the set, and costume sketches and lighting plots and everything, it's always a horrible shock. And I just sit there. I go to some very dark place, where all I see are the things that bother me, and I can't see any of the good things about them. So during the technical rehearsals in San Francisco, I was just trying to stay out of everybody's way. I don't think I even spoke to Joe or anybody for, like, a week, because I knew all I'd say would be complaints and gripes, which is the last thing they needed to hear while they were trying to get this mammoth thing under way. But I was very concerned about whether the show would come off at all.

WINNIE HOLZMAN: I remember the first night we had an audience. Some people came in witch hats! It was a little, um, fanatical, but adorable. Maybe they were fans of the novel or just there in anticipatory witchiness. And the company got through it magnificently. Stephen and I had never seen the whole show. We'd never gotten through an entire run of the show without stopping. So to me, it was a miraculous evening. I remember standing next to Stephen, and we were clutching each other's hands when it started. When the Time Dragon started moving around and doing the smoke thing, the whole audience got excited.

STEPHEN SCHWARTZ: Kristin came down in her bubble, she said her first line—"It's good to see me, isn't it?"—and it got a huge laugh. Winnie and I looked at each other. Then when Idina sang "The Wizard and I," the house came down. We were enormously relieved— even though the show was way too long and there were dead spots and things that clearly weren't working. We could tell from the first preview that the show worked, basically.

KRISTIN CHENOWETH: I knew the minute that Idina and I sang "For Good" that we had something. It was a very special moment, for me, to hear the audience's response. Believe me, I've been in shows where the audience's response wasn't like that. And it was really fun.

IDINA MENZEL: My mom came up to San Francisco, and she would go to the bathroom to hear what the other ladies said about the show—sort of spy on them for her daughter! And she would always tell me how people were so moved by the show. Even at intermission, they were coming in with tears in their eyes. I had the same feeling when I heard the music and read the story. It was just a matter of how to tell it. And it's funny: Developing a musical, it's all a matter of adding, taking away, and testing. You take a song out of the first act and you put it in the second act—all of the sudden there's a weird imbalance. And then you've got to go back to the first act and add a couple of lines that maybe you cut out, but now they don't make sense, because they're out of context. And we actors are learning new lines the morning before we put them up in front of an audience. I'd literally give my dresser little Post-It notes with my lines and she'd read them to me in the wings since I couldn't remember what changed. It was exhilarating. When I look back, it was the hardest time in my life, but the most rewarding one, too.

GREGORY MAGUIRE: A writer's life can be like Emily Dickinson's: intensely private and often very lonely. I came to the first night in San Francisco. I walked in and sat down. Curtain rises. Of course, I'm ready to be fiercely embarrassed and shrink in my seat. Kristin floats down, and she is funny, with that voice of four octaves. Then, Idina comes onstage, rushing to the front in Elphaba's clumsy, ungainly way. Now, Idina has won the Tony Award for best actress, which I think she wildly deserved. And I know she had a big following from *Rent*. But the kind of applause that greeted her was of a different nature. They weren't greeting Idina as a famous singer or actress. About 1,500 people were greeting her as the Wicked Witch of the West. And they were cheering the Witch on. I'll tell you, the hair on the back of my head stood up, and it basically hasn't gone back down again. It was exactly the antithesis of what a writer does, alone, shaping a paragraph, or considering how to pose a moral question in a story. Basically, I have permanent gooseflesh now. It's a medical condition of having a play on Broadway. However many times I see the musical, I still can hardly believe that there are so many people screaming and cheering for the Wicked Witch of the West.

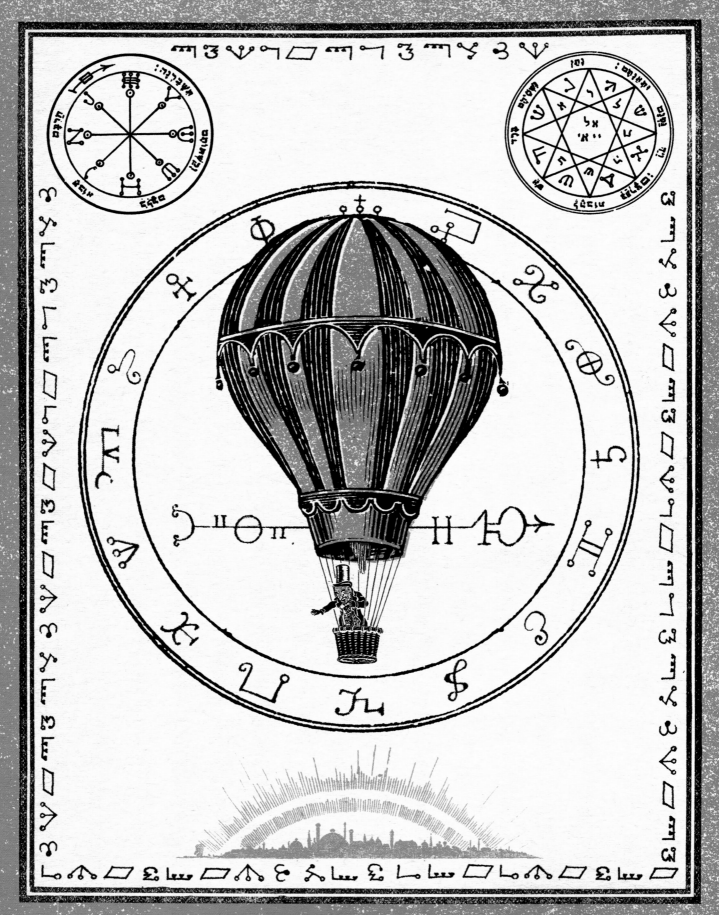

PLATE II.

I was merely blown here / By the winds of chance

Chapter II

WONDERFUL

THE NOVEL UPON WHICH *WICKED* WAS BASED IS A COMPLICATED piece of literature. More than 400 pages of prose tell the story of Elphaba from her birth to her death at the hands of Dorothy, who appears in the last section of the book as a marginal figure. While the world of *Wicked* is faithfully based on L. Frank Baum's world of Munchkins, Winkies, and the Emerald City, author Gregory Maguire adds a religious dimension to the story. He creates an ancient pagan religion called Lurlinism, as well as Unionism, which resembles our world's Protestantism. He introduces the Clock of the Time Dragon as the symbol of a new, bawdy sect known as "the pleasure faith." Maguire's Oz is also a political minefield, in which the Wizard methodically curtails the rights of Animals in order to consolidate his power. In fact, Maguire distinguishes Animals from animals; the former have souls and intelligence, and can speak. Another element of the novel that didn't make it into the musical is the adult situations: The grown-up Elphaba and Fiyero of the novel have a passionate love affair, and Maguire goes into a fair amount of detail.

From beginning to middle to end, the book and the musical deviate substantially, but this is especially true of the end. It's not giving anything away to say that the novel ends on a darker note and does not provide easy definitions of goodness or wickedness. And many of the revelations in the musical *Wicked*—the origins of the Scarecrow and the Tin Woodman, for example—are not to be found in the book. The story of adapting a sprawling novel like *Wicked* is an epic itself. First, one must make a distinction between the "book" of a musical and its score. The book, which Winnie Holzman wrote, includes all the nonmusical scenes; they are, in effect, dramatic or comic scenes that typically provide exposition or push the plot along. The score contains all the songs, which can serve a variety of functions: deepening character, expanding an emotionally significant moment, setting, a mood or even pushing the plot along. Together, the book and score are called the libretto. For the two elements of the libretto, the writers' jobs involved adaptation, both from the source material and to the needs of each element of the musical.

Adaptation has been theater's modus operandi, from the ancient Greeks (they reworked mythology) to Shakespeare (the majority of his plots were taken from published tales). And Broadway musicals have a long and rich history of adaptation: Classics such as *Oklahoma!* and *My Fair Lady* sprang from plays. Today, musicals are created from hit movies (*The Producers*), cartoons (*Beauty and the Beast*), and even collections of pop songs (*Movin' Out*). *Wicked*, adapted from a novel, would require an even more radical alchemical transformation.

*"The trouble with schools is they always try to teach the wrong lesson.
Believe me, I've been kicked out of enough of them to know."*

—FIYERO

Part One

THE WRITE STUFF

F THERE'S ANYONE WRITERS RESPECT, IT'S OTHER WRITERS. FOR A WRITER TO ADAPT ANOTHER'S WORK IS AKIN TO CANNIBALIZING ONESELF. AND YET, EVEN THE MOST REVERENT SCRIBES UNDERSTAND THAT ADAPTATION IS WHAT MAKES THE WORLD GO ROUND. SOME CALL IT INSPIRATION, or creating a composite character from people you know or situations you've been in, but writing is all about transmuting reality into text. Until her involvement with *Wicked*, Winnie Holzman had done original work, mostly in television. She was acclaimed for her writing on the series *thirtysomething* (1987–91) and for the teen drama program she created, *My So-Called Life* (1994–95). Turning a novel into a musical was an entirely new process for her. It was also unfamiliar territory for Gregory Maguire, who had to negotiate the pain and pleasure of seeing his baby turned into a different creature entirely. Stephen Schwartz, on the other hand, was an old hand at the process. After all, he'd already mined the Bible for *Godspell* (1971) and *Children of Eden* (1991).

WINNIE HOLZMAN: Gregory Maguire is an incredible novelist who created a very inspiring world. But after reading the book, I put it aside. I couldn't be too tied to what happened in it. So we sort of stole things that we just had to have. Gregory had the idea that Glinda and Elphaba were roommates in college—that's a knockout idea! At the same time, certain things that were brilliant in the novel wouldn't work in a musical. And I was gravitating right away to more of a love story. The surprise came when it turned out that the love story was about two friends. That wasn't something we knew right away.

GREGORY MAGUIRE: I knew that people would be coming to my novel remembering the 1939 movie. I didn't even need to refer to it much. I could evoke the film with very slender, oblique comments. But I wasn't beholden to it. And why should *Wicked* the musical slavishly conform to my novel, when my novel itself was a playful deviation of the original Baum novel, with glancing references to the movie? I had no problem with Stephen and Winnie taking the material and making it their own. I have a big ego, but it's not *that* big: Let *Wicked* the musical be different than *Wicked* the novel. With my blessing.

WINNIE HOLZMAN: Let's face it: There's nothing harder than the blank page. It's great to have a source that inspires you: a set of relationships, a set of givens. It's a wonderful thing. Obviously, there are pitfalls. I had to let the novel go, but it lived in my mind. I didn't refer to it very often, physically. Once in a while I would, if I needed a name or a place or an image. I remember talking with Stephen early on about creating the sense that the audience was sort of living in a novel springing to life. And even though we didn't use all the little details of plot that Gregory had, we wanted people to feel like they were being told a real story—a story that takes you here and there, with high points, scary moments, and funny moments. To me, that's novelistic.

STEPHEN SCHWARTZ: Once Winnie and I began to work, the plot changed a good deal. Different people have different processes. I'm very structure oriented. And this piece needed to have its structure worked out, because the book is so full of incident and plot. We needed to figure out what story we were going to tell and how. That took a while to outline. Luckily, Winnie is the best rewriter I have ever worked with. I've never encountered anyone with her ability to rethink a scene without losing the essence of it. I've worked with a lot of very talented writers, and when it was time to rewrite, they either tended to just reshuffle the same parts, or they threw everything out—the baby and the bathwater. Winnie has the ability to retain the baby and completely change the bathwater.

WINNIE HOLZMAN: To take one example, the Wizard's character evolved in terms of what we were seeing around us. When we started writing *Wicked* in

STEPHEN SCHWARTZ: Gregory's book is firmly set in Oz, but it parallels events and political situations that we know of on earth, both current and from the more overtly fascist days. We were very aware of them when we wrote. I'm not trying to imply that references in a song like "Popular" are as dark as that, although I think "Wonderful" is pretty dark. Gregory's Oz is basically a fascist society. We didn't push that far—we made it more about American politics. Depending on what color state you live in, you have a view of how close to fascism we are right now. Or not.

MARC PLATT: Of course, the Wizard has no power. He has to exploit the fear and ignorance of others. That is a theme in history that repeats itself over and over. How many times have we seen leaders or dictators who prey on the differences in others in order to galvanize a group of people? It happens all the time in history, repeatedly. That resonates.

THE WIZARD HAS NO POWER. HE HAS TO EXPLOIT THE FEAR AND IGNORANCE OF OTHERS. THAT IS A THEME IN HISTORY THAT REPEATS ITSELF OVER AND OVER.

—MARC PLATT

early 1998, the Bill Clinton scandal had just broken out. Everyone was reeling with the absurdity and horribleness of what we'd all been through with that scandal. And we ended up talking about the Wizard a little bit like Clinton, somebody who had these weaknesses. Then, while we were developing the script, George W. Bush took power. And the Wizard changed. He became more dangerous. We were just responding to what was going on around us. I mean, in the middle of writing, New York City was attacked on September 11. And you would have to have been living under a rock not to see what was going on around you. We already had a story that had to do with power and the nature of using power. We had to ask, "What does it mean to be powerful?"

DAVID STONE: What's fascinating to me is that Gregory wrote the novel in 1995, as a response to the ways in which our government lies to us, from Watergate through the Gulf War. Stephen and Winnie started writing it in the late '90s. And then it became more relevant after September 11 and this particular administration. That is, if you're looking at the political side of it. *Wicked* will always be relevant to people who want to see that aspect. But it's not really time specific. I mean, it's set in another world. Ten years from now, *Wicked* is still going to be *Wicked*.

STEPHEN SCHWARTZ: When I start a show, there are things that I know right away. Part of the show comes fully formed in my head almost

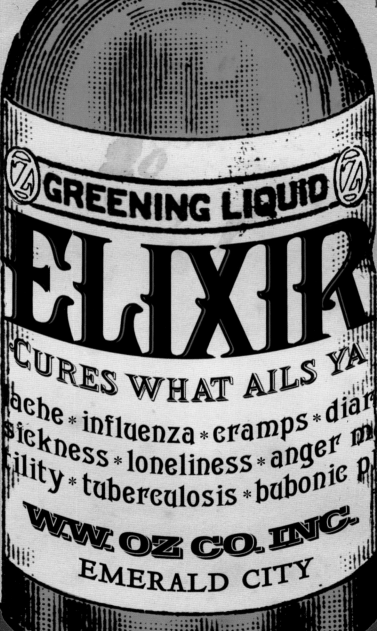

immediately. With *Wicked*, I always knew how it was going to open, how it was going to end, and what the end of the first act would be. I always knew Elphaba would fly at the end of the first act. I didn't know that the song was going to be called "Defying Gravity." But the end of the first act was when she would get on that broom and take off. Having Fiyero become the Scarecrow and Boq the Tin Woodsman was also very important to me from the beginning. In the book, you find out the origin of the Cowardly Lion. Elphaba rescues a cub, and he becomes the Cowardly Lion, which I thought was incredibly cool—so ingenious on Gregory's part. But then I was disappointed: The Tin Woodsman is in the story, but he has no part in the plot. Then in Gregory's book, when Elphaba hears about the Scarecrow, she wonders, Well, that might be Fiyero. But he doesn't turn

out to be Fiyero. So then I thought, well, if he is Fiyero, how did he become the Scarecrow, and what could it possibly have to do with Elphaba? That's when that whole plot began to be devised.

WINNIE HOLZMAN: One of the amazing things about working with Stephen was the vision he had for the entire show. He knew from the very beginning how the show would begin and end. He wanted it to begin with a variation on "Ding Dong, the Witch Is Dead," with the Winkies celebrating Elphaba's death. For the end of the story, he saw Elphaba and Fiyero in the Badlands, healing the Animals who've fled there. Eventually, Joe persuaded us that we didn't need to show that much, so we ended with Elphaba and Fiyero leaving Oz, but you're not quite sure where they're going.

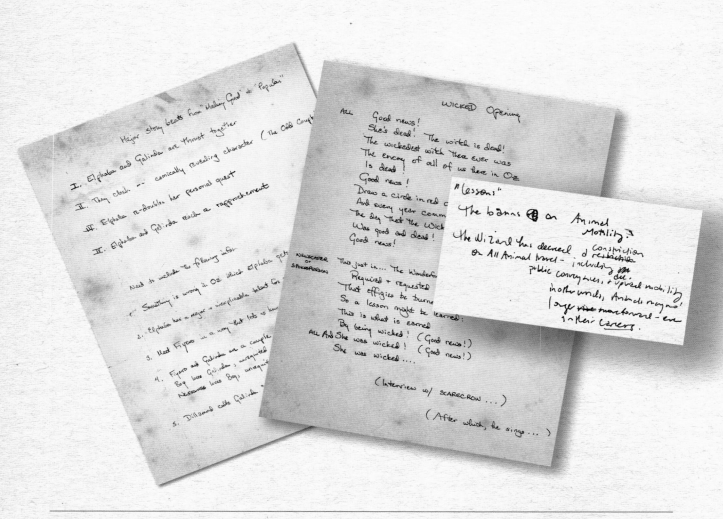

Winnie Holzman's copious notes for Wicked *show her tracking themes through the work, such as "Major story beats" (left) that include "Elphaba and Galinda are thrust together" and "Elphaba re-doubles her personal quest." Another page (center) shows Holzman and Schwartz's initial ideas for the opening number, in which a "Newscaster or Spokesperson" declares the Wicked Witch dead and interviews the Scarecrow. The note card at right shows Holzman jotting down notes about the restriction of Animal rights in Oz.*

WICKED

THE LIFE *and* TIMES *of*
the WICKED WITCH *of the* WEST

By

GREGORY MAGUIRE

On June 9, 1993, Gregory Maguire sat down to pen the initial pages of what, less than two years later, would be the novel upon which *Wicked* was based. Working by hand, the author wielded a roller-point pen (thinnest line possible, black ink) on a closely ruled spiral-bound notebook. According to Maguire: "When I get a few pages, I transcribe them onto the computer, and sometimes, in the act of transcription, my creative energy is prompted further." Read side by side, the raw manuscript pages and the printed text bear striking similarities and differences. Here you can see the novelist's mind at work: crossing out words or scribbling added phrases in the margins. Above, an original depiction of Elphaba, painted by Gregory Maguire. ❧

"I think today's the day," said the wife, pressing her hands lightly down, smoothing the ~~belly of her~~ nightdress around the world she carried inside her. "I do think it'll be today. Look how low I've gone." ~~inconvenient~~

"~~It~~ ~~Today, that~~ would be like you, perverse and ~~thoughtless, today~~," said the husband, standing at the doorway ~~and~~ looking outwards, over the lake ~~they had been gray, outlines a few moments ago~~ the far fields, the forested hills. They grew in definition and resolve as the sun climbed. You could just make out the chimneys of Fog Hollow, breakfast fires smoking. "The worst possible moment for my ministry."

The wife, normally resigned, merely yawned and ~~three~~ tightened her lips around her teeth, tucking them together, biting the inside ridge. As if in rehearsal for facial expressions later on. "I do think you bear half the blame of the lousy timing," she said lightly. "I mean, after all, Frex."

"That's how the thinking goes, but I wonder," said the husband.

"You wonder?" She laughed, her head going far back. The line from her ear, along her chin, to the hollow below her throat ~~looked like~~ ~~reminded Frex of~~ an elegant silver ladle. Even in morning disarray, with a belly like a ~~royal barge~~ scow ~~scow~~, she was majestically good-looking.○ "You mean, – she began to work her legs over to the bed's edge — "you wonder – " and out ~~like~~ straight, wriggling her toes — "if you're the father – " grabbing the bedstead; Frex grabbed her other arm and hauled — "or the ~~general~~ fatherliness of men in general?" Then she was standing, a whole promontory alive and mobile, an ambulatory island, a small comet plunged to earth and slowed down by gravity but resiliently independent. She blazed out the door in slow motion, laughing at such a conceit on what might be her first child's birthday, and he could hear her laughing from the outhouse even as he began to dress for the day's battle.

○ ~~Why couldn't it remind him of a flower, or a holy thing, a chalice for burning propitiating oils?~~ It irked him that ~~she~~ even in her body she spoke of privilege. He blamed her for it even while admiring her efforts to overcome her highborn advantages.

Frex combed his beard and oiled his scalp. With one hand he drew his lion's mane back and with the other he fastened a clasp of bone and rawhide to keep his face free ~~of~~. His expressions today must be readable from across the village center. There could be no fuzziness of meaning. So some coal dust to darken his eyes, a smear of red wax on his flat cheeks. He tried, and then removed, shade on his lips.

In the kitchen yard Philmaray was moving gently, not with the heaviness of freighted women but as if inflated, a huge balloon trailing its strings through the dirt. She bobbed, she paused, she floated on, a skillet in one hand and a few eggs and the whiskery tips of autumn chives in the other. She sang to herself, but only in short phrases. Frex wasn't meant to hear. He reckoned singing among the more suspicious talents and he preached against it, but only now and then. Selecting his robe from the clothes press, he chose this morning to let her sing. He had a bigger ~~every battle~~ to fight today than his wife, and if she was going to drop the baby today she could be allowed that little liberty.

But when his mendicant's gown was buttoned tight to the neck, and his ~~boots laced on over squirming feet~~, sandals strapped on over the ~~modest~~ wrappings on his calves (to insure modesty) Frex took up the pages of report sent him from his fellow divines' over in Three Dead Trees, several day's ride away. He went to the dooryard and read it aloud — not so much for Philmaray, who had already heard it six times — but for himself, to put himself in fighting form, to stir his blood to readiness.

Philmaray dangled a wooden spoon in the skillet and stirred eggs as she read. One hand went out to rest on her hip. She looked like a big-bellied china pitcher with a flourish for a handle and a long sinuous spout. Beyond, the hills proved once again to be made of individual, separate trees, ~~biting their~~ spiked and globe-shaped, broad and narrow, green and gray-green and brown-green in the lifting haze. The tinkle of cow bells sounded across the lake.

A week or two later ~~Boq took his one~~ afternoon off, Boq took himself in to Railway Square. ~~At~~ a kiosk selling cigarettes, ~~awings of~~ naughty women, and ~~religious~~ scrolls ~~elabora featuring hillside~~ ~~paintings~~ of skyscrapes ~~overloaded~~ with one-line religious slogans. ("Lurline isn't Gone; She Lives Within Each Heart." "Keep the Wizard's Laws, and the Laws Will Keep You Safe." "I Pray to the Nameless God, That Justice Will Walk in Oz." Boq observed the pagan, the ~~total~~ totalitarian, and the old-fashioned unionist impulses in what was offered to the public, and thought briefly how strange what was not on display: anything encouraging ~~to~~ either tiktokist or ~~pleasure faith sen plaither magic~~ magic ~~(plea~~ plaither sensibilities, which seemed in his limited _____ to be ~~too strongest~~ social forces at work these days, both in Gillikin and back home in Munchkinland. Perhaps they were so well entrenched that the populace didn't need convincing by banners and cross-stitch samplers. Anyway, it didn't surprise him that there was no ~~thin~~ directly sympathetic to the ~~royalists~~, who had surely gone underground in the harsh fifteen years since the Wizard ~~first~~ wrested power from the Ozma Regent. The

Part Two

CHARACTER IS DESTINY

WHEN ACTORS OPEN A SCRIPT AND START TO READ THEIR LINES, THEY MAY IMMEDIATELY SEE THEMSELVES, OR A VERSION OF THEMSELVES, OR SOMETHING THEY WORRY THEY COULD NEVER ATTAIN. YOU MAY HAVE HEARD ABOUT "METHOD ACTORS," BUT THE TRUTH IS THAT every performer has an individualized method of approaching and realizing a role. Some start from the outside, imagining the clothes and makeup the character might have, and thereby finding the character from an external process. Others start by digging deep within themselves, finding memories or sensations that correspond to the characters' and thus working toward emotional honesty in the performance. Still others use a little of everything, building their characters piece by piece and consulting closely with the writer and director to arrive at a unique creation. The original Broadway cast members of *Wicked* each left his or her stamp on the characters (even though it's up to each successive performer to make it distinctive). Acting is a notoriously elusive art to analyze or explain, but here, some *Wicked* veterans reveal their methods.

IDINA MENZEL
{*on playing Elphaba*}

AS FAR AS building a character, I don't have a set process. I study the text and go by what the playwright is saying. And, as soon as you put on the green makeup and the black dress, it brings another whole dimension. But generally, in rehearsals, I just tried to go on my own personal experience and make everything specific. I find that if you do it the other way—build a character starting from external aspects—you can miss what the playwright is really saying. The outside stuff is easy. But I like to take it slow with the text first, and then start adding on other character details. Obviously, one of the big things about the show is the friendship between Elphaba and Glinda. Girls have a harder time keeping their friendships for some reason, especially when they're both gifted. I love how each desires what the other one has. Deep down, Elphaba would much rather look like Glinda and have her charisma and popularity. And I think that Glinda gets a lot from Elphaba: she becomes more honest with herself. I don't know if I ever had a friendship like that.

SHOSHANA BEAN
{*on playing Elphaba*}

I'VE NEVER DONE anything consciously to make my performance or interpretation different, because I admired Idina's performance so much. If anything, I wanted to emulate it and do justice to what she had created. But, just by nature, what I try to do is bring a lot of myself to whatever I'm doing, character-wise. I grew up a Jewish girl in Oregon, and those years were hard. A lot of my friends were those cute, skinny little blond girls, and I was a thicker, ethnic, mouthy girl. So, I definitely had my run-ins with the boys a lot. Mostly they were the football players who gave me the most crap. So, there's a lot of Shoshana in Elphaba. I move around a lot. I'm very energetic, and I'm very active and I'm very feisty. Idina's still and regal. I definitely throw my energy out there a lot. I came into *Wicked* straight off the heels of being in *Hairspray*. It was funny, because the production supervisor of *Wicked* was our stage manager at *Hairspray*. So when he was putting me into the show, he was like, Shoshana, this is not *Hairspray*. You cannot stand like a 16-year-old. I was like, I know, I know! I've been playing a 16-year-old for two years now. I do love being able to bring that to the young Elphaba. And then I get to play her when she's older—and fierce!

STEPHANIE J. BLOCK
{on playing Elphaba}

ELPHABA'S STORY is one that anyone who has been judged by outward appearances can understand. She's ostracized because of her appearance. She's just trying to make the right choices and live a passionate life. I relate to that struggle a lot. As soon as I heard Stephen's music, I so wanted to be a part of this project. And when it was making its journey to Broadway, it just wasn't my time. I understudied Idina in San Francisco and went on once, but I wasn't able to do the Broadway run. And that was literally my cry, "Oh, my gosh, but I just want it! You know, I just want it!" And that's very much what Elphaba is, she has all of these talents and hopes and dreams, and she wants to make them come to fruition, but all these outward things are getting in her way. There's the idea of feeling lonely, feeling different, and I think any actor could recognize that in him- or herself. To go out onstage and want 3,000 people applauding you, there is a definite need for acceptance! And, to get

more personal, when I was younger, I had tons of issues with my physical appearance. So when I sing "I'm Not That Girl," it really hits a button in me—I have to hold back tears because it hits a chord with me like no other song I've ever sung before.

KRISTIN CHENOWETH
{on playing Glinda}

GLINDA IS A VERY complicated character. There are lots of layers that I tried to reveal. Act I is so fun, because there she is: the girl that we love to look at and say, "Oh, we know her." But Act II unfolds, and she's a totally different person. Mainly, I was concentrating on creating a performance that was more than just bitchy. I wanted to see an evolution happen. All Glinda wants is to be the first lady and to have her prince. And in her way, she tries to help Elphaba in "Popular." That is her way of being nice; I never wanted it to be condescending. I wanted it to be like, "I really want to help you become prettier." Then there are the romantic layers. All of us have been through a broken heart. Glinda falls hard for Fiyero. And in Act II, she starts to realize that he is not really in love with her. How many times have we been in a relationship and we think, "We're together right now, but he or she is not really with me?" Glinda's worst nightmare comes true when Fiyero falls in love with Elphaba, her best friend. One thing that Joe Mantello did that was so brilliant, I thought, was to have Glinda stand at the side of the stage, watching Elphaba melt. It's a great moment for both characters. It's a scene that we know so well, but never before would you think that Glinda is watching that. And her heart is broken because she knows that she basically set Elphaba up to be killed. In the end, Glinda carries on in a totally different way. She gets to be queen, but she has learned something and grown. It's like when you get a little knocked around and you have some edginess to you. *Wicked* is about love, acceptance, and forgiveness. I think that is why it appeals to so many people.

JENNIFER LAURA THOMPSON
{on playing Glinda}

TAKING OVER THE role from Kristin—who was so brilliant—was daunting, and I didn't want to copy her. So I tried to make Glinda my own by listening to my instincts and what the script was telling me. I've done comic roles before, like in *Urinetown,* and I think there's a danger in hearing so much laughter. That's the balance I struggle with on a daily basis, trying not to go over the top, so I don't end up creating a caricature of myself. But I can still fall into a trap of enjoying the laughter and trying to get more laughs out of the audience. I'm constantly pulling in the reins! As for building character, Glinda is probably a piece of many different people I've met in my life. Unlike Kristin, I certainly am not a pageant girl. I tended to go with Glinda's awkwardness, or goofiness, rather than an image of perfection. In my teenage years, I felt more like Elphaba than Glinda. So, even though I play Glinda, that part of the story is very important to me. And, examining it from the other side, to play someone who was the most popular, the most beautiful, is interesting. I have to give a heart and soul to the sort of person who, as a child, I never thought cared about anything.

KENDRA KASSEBAUM
{on playing Glinda}

SIMPLY PUT, I think Glinda is trying to find her truth. She came from a very privileged world. It's not ugly; it's the only way she knows. And she encounters people on her journey who open her eyes to what's out there. She grows on the journey. When we first meet her, Glinda may be a bit of a snob, but I think it's an innocent snobbery. I mean, in the Upper Uplands—where she's from—that's the behavior she saw. That's how you act and present yourself: You're flawless and that makes the world a better place. But my job is to make her character deeper as the show progresses. That's the challenge during rehearsals. It's about finding the truth in the story, never playing for the laughs. With Glinda, there's innocence about her and I think that's where the humor lies. The way the character is so perfectly formed in the show, it's kind of hard to mess it up. You get to come down in this huge bubble, wearing a princess costume. But there is a trap to Glinda. You don't want to play the falseness of her, because she's true to the core.

JOEL GREY
{on playing the Wonderful Wizard of Oz}

WHEN JOE AND Winnie and Stephen contacted me about playing the Wizard on Broadway, I had a long conversation with them, because I didn't have a clear focus on the character: why he did what he did and who he was as a human being. The other characters are more thoroughly investigated, especially the girls. And they talked about the Wizard wanting to be a father and take care of everybody in Oz. Being a dad is something I'm very familiar with. So we worked to deepen the psychological aspects of the Wizard. I saw him as a convenient politician. Personally, I didn't think of him as such a bad guy, whereas in the novel, he's actually quite evil. But he's not the villain of *Wicked.* If there is one, it's Madame Morrible. I mean, she's a flat-out bad person! I saw the Wizard as pure in a way, and ultimately, a man just trying to survive. Another thing that got me very interested was the complexity of the Act II number, "Wonderful," even though it's in the guise of a soft-shoe vaudeville routine. Before opening on Broadway, we totally rethought that song. I knew it needed something more to take off, and I had this idea that the Wizard loved Elphaba so much, but never realized that she's his daughter. His connection with her was very important. In that scene, she's so dark and angry and thinks the Wizard is such a bad guy, I just had to charm her somehow. So I get her to dance with me. And dance with joy.

GEORGE HEARN
{on playing the Wonderful Wizard of Oz}

IT'S A VERY interesting character, very rich. Richer in the book than in the film. It's nuanced by the darkness of the novel, the writing. Mainly, he's a person who thinks he's right about everything. He tries to win the crowds over by playing the huckster, drawling in a slight, charming Western accent. But he thinks he's right, so he says, "I want to make everybody happy." He's like the president that way, like many other presidents. He wants to do the right thing. But if you don't go along with the plan, you could end up in jail. So the play gets down to the nuts and bolts of what makes a society work. It also reminds me of the ancient Greek tragedy *Antigone* a lot. You know, Creon wants to do the practical thing to keep control of his power. And Antigone says, "I don't care. I'm the idealist." So the Wizard is a wonderful character to play, and I don't think he ever feels that he's being sinister or evil.

DAVID GARRISON
{on playing the Wonderful Wizard of Oz}

THE WIZARD is a man of limited talent who finds himself in a position of great power through no particular act of his own. The only way to hold on to power is to convince people that they ought to be afraid of something. But of course like all good villains, he doesn't think of himself as the villain. Everybody in the show, to a certain extent, is swimming in those morally dangerous waters, but it's Elphaba who makes the ethical choice. From an acting standpoint, I'm conceiving of the Wizard like the legendary song-and-dance men on Broadway, like George M. Cohan. That's appropriate to the character, because he's basically a con man, so you want a little flim-flam, you want a little song and dance. You want a physical manifestation of his personality. And the Wizard really does have the charm to seduce.

CAROLE SHELLEY
{on playing Madame Morrible}

I'M ENGLISH. At least, I was. I've been in America for 40-odd years. If they pay me enough I can keep the accent. I didn't want to make Madame Morrible traditionally evil. I wanted [her evilness] to be a surprise. Evil people seem perfectly normal, until the day that they deem fit to display the other side. In some ways, my character is a plot-moving machine. I can't think about it that way. I mean, I don't set out to be a machine, I set out to be Morrible, and that's simply what she does. During rehearsals and the San Francisco tryouts, my performance got more and more expressive. Quite frequently, Joe would tell me to make Morrible "bigger." Also, I have a secret about my character that I can't tell you: It has to do with the strange noises and sounds Morrible makes. Tom Watson designed and made my wigs and we discussed how Morrible's look would change through the show. I thought as she got more evil, her hairline should recede. And that seemed to work very well. Ultimately, of course, Morrible comes to a bad end. She's probably locked up somewhere in the Emerald City. The Wizard and I think it would be kind of fun if they both ran off together and lived somewhere quietly, in Oklahoma.

CAROL KANE
{on playing Madame Morrible}

MADAME MORRIBLE is a genius Headmistress. But she also has sorcery know-how, enough to see magical talent when she sees it. And she has excellent control of the weather; she's the one who causes the house to fall and kill the Wicked Witch of the East. Morrible starts out with an average job that she has done very well for a long time, but with no advancement. When she discovers Elphaba's genius, her ambitions change. She sees a way to become part of this glorious new Oz the Wizard is creating, so she lays her bricks of gold, as it were, to get up that tower. Madame Morrible is a juicy character. As a performer, I think she has a good character arc. Also, for me, it's an extremely challenging project, because I've never been in a musical before—at least, as a grownup. I did play a Munchkin in a school production of *The Wizard of Oz* when I was a kid in Ohio, but nothing since then. As an adult, I sang "professionally" in a movie called *The Lemon Sisters*, but my singing had to be so bad, Nathan Lane comes to watch my act in Atlantic City and offers me a gig at a comedy club. But I am trying to sing well this time around! I have been studying. Still, Joe Mantello said to me in rehearsal, "Why don't you just speak it?"

NORBERT LEO BUTZ
{on playing Fiyero}

GETTING FIYERO RIGHT was tricky for everyone involved. He's the male romantic lead of the show, but he's also part of a love triangle. In the novel, the triangle doesn't exist, and Fiyero and Elphaba meet much later, as adults out of school, living their lives and meeting almost as strangers. In the play we have the messy he-loves-her, she-loves-him, she-loves-him-too structure, and, to add even more confusion to the mix, the real love story is between the two ladies. So, *who is this guy* became the overwhelming question. He couldn't be just eye candy, because that would be reductive to the leading women—especially to Elphaba, whom we have to believe is such a smart, intuitive, and painfully sensitive young woman. I played soccer as a kid, and I had to work my ass off to even make a team, let alone play. Fiyero reminded me of so many guys I played soccer with who were just effortlessly talented. They never seemed to sweat, looked great in their uniforms and seamlessly went from gorgeous girl to gorgeous girl. But the writers did something really smart before we opened in New York: They gave Fiyero the slightest trace of a conscience, a longing that something more important was to be gotten out of life. In the lion cub scene he says "I happen to be genuinely self-absorbed and deeply shallow," to joke his way out of a confrontation with Elphaba. She replies, "No. You're not. Or you wouldn't be so unhappy." It's a great moment because the audience gets to see his mask fall to the floor, and in that moment he falls hopelessly in love with the green girl. To me, the play is all about transformation: how we grow into the people we become and what masks and relationships we have to drop along the way.

DAVID AYERS
{on playing Fiyero}

CONSIDERING that Fiyero is a vehicle to tell the story of the two women, he's still really interesting. I mean, he's not horrifically one-dimensional. He has a cool journey, which I think is very similar to the journey the audience takes. In the beginning, the audience sees Elphaba, and they're like, "Whoa, she's green! Who is this person?" And by the end of the play, they're rooting for her and they've fallen in love with her, the way Fiyero does. The two journeys mirror each other. I think the audience identifies with Fiyero in that he has this cathartic breakthrough. It starts in the lion cub scene when Fiyero and Elphaba steal the cage together, that's the catalyst. The turning point is when Elphaba tells him he only pretends that he's shallow and self-absorbed—otherwise, he wouldn't be so unhappy. That deeply affects him. And that was the note I always got in rehearsals from Joe. There has to be a moment when he's rattled and unsure of himself. Because, come on, Fiyero is a Winkie prince and no one has ever spoken to him like that. There are all sorts of layers in that scene; he's never been alone in the woods with someone like this. And Elphaba is yelling and ordering him around, like, "Don't shake the cage, don't do this, what are you doing?" They're practically having a lovers' spat. And that's the way love can start.

DERRICK WILLIAMS
{on playing Fiyero}

I BASICALLY TRIED to make Fiyero the kind of person who doesn't have a care in the world. He's had it easy in life. He is a bit spoiled and usually gets what he wants. I based him a little on the character Will Smith played in *The Fresh Prince of Bel-Air*. What drives this character is the knowledge that he can get away with anything. Whether it's getting the girl he wants, skipping school, or even getting expelled, he won't get in trouble for it. But later in the show, things change. Fiyero realizes the things he truly wants in life and starts doing things necessary to have them. I personally think I bring something totally different to the role. I think the difference between myself and Norbert Leo Butz is pretty obvious and we both add our own flavor to it, which makes it both different and unique.

CHRISTOPHER FITZGERALD
{on playing Boq}

I TRIED TO CHART Boq's journey through the show, even though *Wicked* is really about Elphaba and Glinda. But it was fun to have this little guy around with one clear goal in mind: his faithful love for Glinda. There's so much music and story, it was a challenge to clarify those moments so you can understand what's going on with Boq and how he gets involved with Nessarose and she latches onto him. I think it's kind of sad, that whole Boq and Nessarose subplot. Ultimately he wants to do the right thing, and his way of staying connected to Glinda is, strangely enough, taking care of Nessarose. Boq isn't a traditional Munchkin, as we know them from the books or movie. There was a line early on when Glinda would say, "Aren't you a little tall for a Munchkin?" and I'd be like, "Yeah, I don't wanna brag…" Or I'd say I was half-Munchkin, half-Winkie. The really tough part was putting on the silver makeup and the prosthetic nose and chin for the Act II transformation. That could be rough on the skin. Although, I must admit, the producers of the show paid for me to get facials every two weeks. So that was a nice experience.

JEFFREY KUHN
{on playing Boq}

WHAT'S STRUCTURALLY difficult about the show is taking this epic novel and distilling it. Even more challenging is the fact that these secondary characters like Boq and Nessarose have to fulfill storytelling functions, sometimes at the expense of being drawn-out characters. Boq on stage is very different from Boq in the book. All of the characters' thwarted desires, their unrequited loves, manifest in different ways. Boq is denied access to Glinda and an opportunity to profess his love for her because of what happens to Elphaba. That boils into this hatred of Elphaba and a single-minded pursuit of destroying her. Nessarose's unrequited love for Boq causes her to destroy him by turning him into the Tin Woodman. Everyone's desires lead to the tragic elements of the story. What's worse than unrequited love, really? Certainly, Boq performs some basic comic relief functions. But he also has a sweet little story. It's quite a heartbreaking journey he goes on.

LOGAN LIPTON
{on playing Boq}

IN BOQ, WINNIE and Stephen have written a boy who goes from having the largest heart in Oz, to none at all. I didn't realize this fact at the beginning of the rehearsal process. I was toying with the idea that his main concern was just to keep Fiyero from Galinda, so I started to develop a strange animosity for Fiyero. Only later did I find that Boq's main concern was Galinda, period. To make Boq's journey broader, his initial actions all had to be driven with a genuine desire to be loved. It makes his ultimate transformation into the angry, vengeful Tin Woodsman that much more tragic. At one time or another, we've all been victims of unrequited love. And we all know what that feels like. It makes you do drastic and sometimes ridiculous things. So if the character is based on anyone, it's based on me—an unloved, stalker-like me who went to great lengths to get the attention of someone I thought I loved. But that is one of the strange aspects of the role. I would be willing to bet that if Boq spent more than 20 seconds at a time with this egomaniacal, self-satisfied sorority chick, he would see Galinda for what she really is. His love may feel genuine, but it's an unattainable one. Isn't the anticipation of the catch more gratifying than the catch itself?

MICHELLE FEDERER
{on playing Nessarose}

I FEEL A LOT of empathy for Nessarose. In rehearsals, I could really identify with her. I was stuck in the wheelchair for eight hours. I didn't know anyone in the cast. It was my first Broadway show. So I was nervous, and I spent a lot of time sitting in that wheelchair, and I felt pretty isolated. But I just went with it, because it was right for the part. I found that if I really wanted to be heard about something, I had to stand up and get out of the wheelchair, to be included in conversations. So I understood that Nessarose wants so badly to be something other than what she is. And she does crazy things to make that happen. In Act II, when this miracle happens and she can walk, she thinks it's all going to be fine, but it all falls apart. She's desperate to be normal and loved, even though it's obvious that Boq doesn't really love her. She's young, not emotionally smart—she doesn't have the benefit of Oprah! This boy, Boq, once asked her to a dance. It's the first time in her life she felt included and normal. She had a pretty pink dress on. And he was genuinely sweet. He told her she was beautiful. That can happen to people—they get stuck in a moment.

JENNA LEIGH GREEN
{on playing Nessarose}

I REALLY HAD to approach Nessarose my own way. Michelle Federer has done a wonderful job creating the part, but we couldn't be more different—physically and in terms of our acting styles. I couldn't even have tried to be the same. I think of my Nessa as softer. Michelle's very determined, and her Nessa sort of stays at a distance from her sister and everyone else. I wanted to see if, in Act I, Nessa could try harder to fit in with everyone else. She's very naïve and wide-eyed. She loves her sister very much. But she is also terribly afraid. She has a disability and worries that people will think she's weird. She's afraid of having more weirdness thrust upon her due to having a green sister. At the same time, she's very, very close with her sister, who has taken care of her every step of the way. Between Acts I and II, about two years have passed. Nessarose is only 20 years old. Her father has died and her sister has disappeared. She had to leave school and now she has to govern Munchkinland. It's all too much for her. So she resents her sister intensely for leaving her. It has made her hard. And she's in love with Boq, who's not in love with her, but because she has power, she can make him do whatever she wants. Using power is the only thing she knows how to do.

WILLIAM YOUMANS
{on playing Dr. Dillamond}

OF COURSE, THE novel is very different from the musical: Doctor Dillamond dies in it. But you could almost argue that what happens to him in *Wicked* is a fate worse than death: He has to go on living, but loses his power of speech and reasoning and becomes just an animal. As for creating the character, I did collect pictures of goats. I even keep some taped to the mirror on my makeup table! But generally, I think of the character as a bit like John Gielgud, only with horns: an avuncular, professorial type in a tweedy three-piece suit from old black-and-white movies. And Dillamond really loves his students. A big part of getting into character is the makeup. I do it myself and it takes about seven minutes. I'm in the opening number, and then I come running back to my dressing room, put on my costume, put on the mask, and then draw on some lines. Then I put on a beard and sideburns. I try to cover up the mask. Other than that, I have a lot of time backstage to reflect. It's pretty clear that Dr. Dillamond represents the Jews

in World War II: You know, being forced from his profession first, and then gradually marginalized, and then finally imprisoned and abused. Anyway, that's hinted at in our show, but that's way too dark for a show that's a comedy. One of the great things about *Wicked*—and Joe Mantello is a master at this—is the way it changes tone abruptly. It'll be very dark one minute, and then suddenly there'll be a funny joke, like, "There's a Goat on the lam." It switches back and forth really deftly, I think. There is a dark side to *Wicked*, and I'm pretty much at the center of it.

TIMOTHY BRITTEN PARKER
{on playing Dr. Dillamond}

DOCTOR DILLAMOND really feels a kinship and connection to Elphaba, since they both understand what it is to be an outsider. From their first scene together, we learn that outside forces are conspiring against both of them—taunting them, pushing them, trying to make them back down. With Elphaba it's her classmates. With Doctor Dillamond it is what's written on the chalkboard: "ANIMALS SHOULD BE SEEN AND NOT HEARD." It's a small part, but crucial, since it's the catalyst for Elphaba to meet the Wizard and save the Animals. A big acting challenge is wearing the goat's head! Essentially, my entire face and body are covered by the costume and mask. I wear cloven hooves on my hands and feet, and part of my work as an actor is getting used to that. I didn't actually go and study any goats to prepare for the role. In my opinion, it's more effective since Dillamond becomes more of a Goat in the Act II scene, when Elphaba discovers him at the Wizard of Oz's palace. At that point, he can't talk anymore. There is a very strong part of him that is humanlike. My feeling is that it's more important that, initially, the audience see his humanlike side more than his goat side. Doctor Dillamond takes great pride in being a Goat, but he speaks and reasons as a teacher. I think that's why it's so sad to see him lose those very important qualities.

"You know black is this year's pink!"

—Glinda (Galinda)

A PRIMER

of the CURIOUS *and*

INCREDIBLE INHABITANTS

of

If personality can be caught in the flash of a bulb,
the photographs that follow do the impossible: capture the
essence of performers and their characters.

ELPHABA

{ LATER, THE WICKED WITCH OF THE WEST }

HISTORIOGRAPHICAL HIGHLIGHTS

Elphaba's origins are shrouded in mystery, but we do know that her mother received a strange visitor before she was born. At Shiz University, Elphaba was a brilliant student with magical gifts that she tried to hide. Because of her green skin, the students, including her roommate, Galinda, shunned her. Elphaba's momentous meeting with the Wizard in the Emerald City set her on the fateful path whereby she became Wicked. ❧

HAILS FROM WHICH OZ PROVINCE	FREQUENTLY SEEN WITH
Munchkinland	Flying broom and *The Grimmerie* tucked under one arm
DEFINISH DEMEANOR	**SIGNATURE UTTERANCE**
Green skin, black hat, quick wit, and the ability to defy gravity	*"I'm the other daughter, Elphaba. I'm beautifully tragic."*

PRIMUS PRINCIPIA PHILOSOPHICA

"Nobody in all of Oz, no Wizard that there is or was, is ever gonna bring me down!"

IDINA MENZEL

(*Original Broadway cast, opposite. Photographed by Henry Leutwyler.*)

GALINDA

{ LATER, GLINDA THE GOOD }

HISTORIOGRAPHICAL HIGHLIGHTS

Galinda couldn't have had a happier upbringing in the Upper Uplands. She was the ideal of golden girlhood—perfectly dressed and poised—to which everyone else aspired. At Shiz University, rooming with the artichoke-colored and bad-tempered Elphaba challenged Glinda's good will. However, the two eventually became friends . . . then enemies. Glinda (who changed her name in deference to Doctor Dillamond, who always mispronounced it) joined forces with the Wizard and Madame Morrible, who unilaterally declared Elphaba Wicked. But Glinda ultimately saw the truth about Elphaba.

HAILS FROM WHICH OZ PROVINCE	FREQUENTLY SEEN WITH
Upper Uplands of Gillikin	Wand, bubbles, and a tiara
DEFINISH DEMEANOR	**SIGNATURE UTTERANCE**
Perfect blond coif, spotless shimmering dress, unutterable beauty, and innate goodness	*"It's good to see me, isn't it?"*

PRIMUS PRINCIPIA PHILOSOPHICA

"It's all about popular."

KRISTIN CHENOWETH

(Original Broadway cast, opposite. Photographed by Henry Leutwyler.)

MADAME MORRIBLE

✣ HISTORIOGRAPHICAL HIGHLIGHTS ✣

When we first meet her, Madame Morrible is the Headmistress at Shiz University. There, she's an eccentric but likeable den mother to the students. She teaches sorcery to Galinda and Elphaba. However, Madame Morrible makes a startling career move when she becomes the Wonderful Wizard of Oz's press secretary. She amasses great power, which, of course, she abuses mightily. Part of Madame Morrible's diabolical propagandizing includes labeling Elphaba "Wicked." ✌

HAILS FROM WHICH OZ PROVINCE	FREQUENTLY SEEN WITH
Unknown—Madame Morrible's origins are shrouded in lies and secrecy.	A scary scowl upon her face and increasingly outrageous outfits

DEFINISH DEMEANOR	SIGNATURE UTTERANCE
Hair pulled back in an extremely tight bun, formal dress with enormous bustle, and enough makeup to send Queen Elizabeth I reaching for the cold cream.	*"Weather is my specialty."*

✣ PRIMUS PRINCIPIA PHILOSOPHICA ✣

"Never apologize for talent! Talent is a gift!
And that is my special talent, encouraging talent."

CAROLE SHELLEY

(Original Broadway cast, opposite. Photographed by Henry Leutwyler.)

THE WIZARD

HISTORIOGRAPHICAL HIGHLIGHTS

Not a lot is known of the Wizard's life before he came to Oz by hot-air balloon, but once here, he certainly made an impression. Before Elphaba was born, he paid her mother a visit. Then, elevated to Wonderful Wizardship of Oz, he added showbiz panache to the Emerald City and started restricting Animal rights. Crossing paths with Elphaba was the beginning of the Wizard's downfall. Exploiting *The Grimmerie* and Elphaba's magical powers, he tricks her into giving his Monkey servant, Chistery, wings.

HAILS FROM WHICH OZ PROVINCE	FREQUENTLY SEEN WITH
None. The Wizard came to Oz in a great balloon from another world. He is often heard to mutter "Kansas" under his breath.	His amazing and fearsome "Wizard head," also a mysterious vial of green liquid
DEFINISH DEMEANOR	**SIGNATURE UTTERANCE**
Lab coat, slippers, and a bemused expression	*"Everyone deserves a chance to fly."*

PRIMUS PRINCIPIA PHILOSOPHICA

"Where I'm from, we believe all sorts of things that aren't true. We call it—'history.'"

JOEL GREY

(Original Broadway cast, opposite. Photographed by Henry Leutwyler.)

CHISTERY

HISTORIOGRAPHICAL HIGHLIGHTS

Chistery is the Wizard's Monkey servant in the Emerald City. Due to a devious piece of trickery, the Wizard arranges for Elphaba to read a spell from the *Grimmerie* that endows Chistery and his fellow Monkeys with unnatural wings. It's a painful process, but it gives them amazing flying powers. After Chistery's falling out with the Wizard, he allies himself with Elphaba, now known as the Wicked Witch of the West.

HAILS FROM WHICH OZ PROVINCE

Chistery initially lives in the Wizard's palace in the Emerald City, but he ends up serving the Wicked Witch at Kiamo Ko castle in Winkie Country.

FREQUENTLY SEEN WITH

The Grimmerie and the other Flying Monkeys

DEFINISH DEMEANOR

Red–black skin and huge wings

SIGNATURE UTTERANCE

Chistery has struggled with gaining speech his entire life.

PRIMUS PRINCIPIA PHILOSOPHICA

Being a Monkey and a servant most of his life, Chistery's philosophical principles are not terribly complex. Like any sentient Animal, though, he wants his freedom.

MANUEL HERRERA

(Original Broadway cast, opposite. Photographed by Henry Leutwyler.)

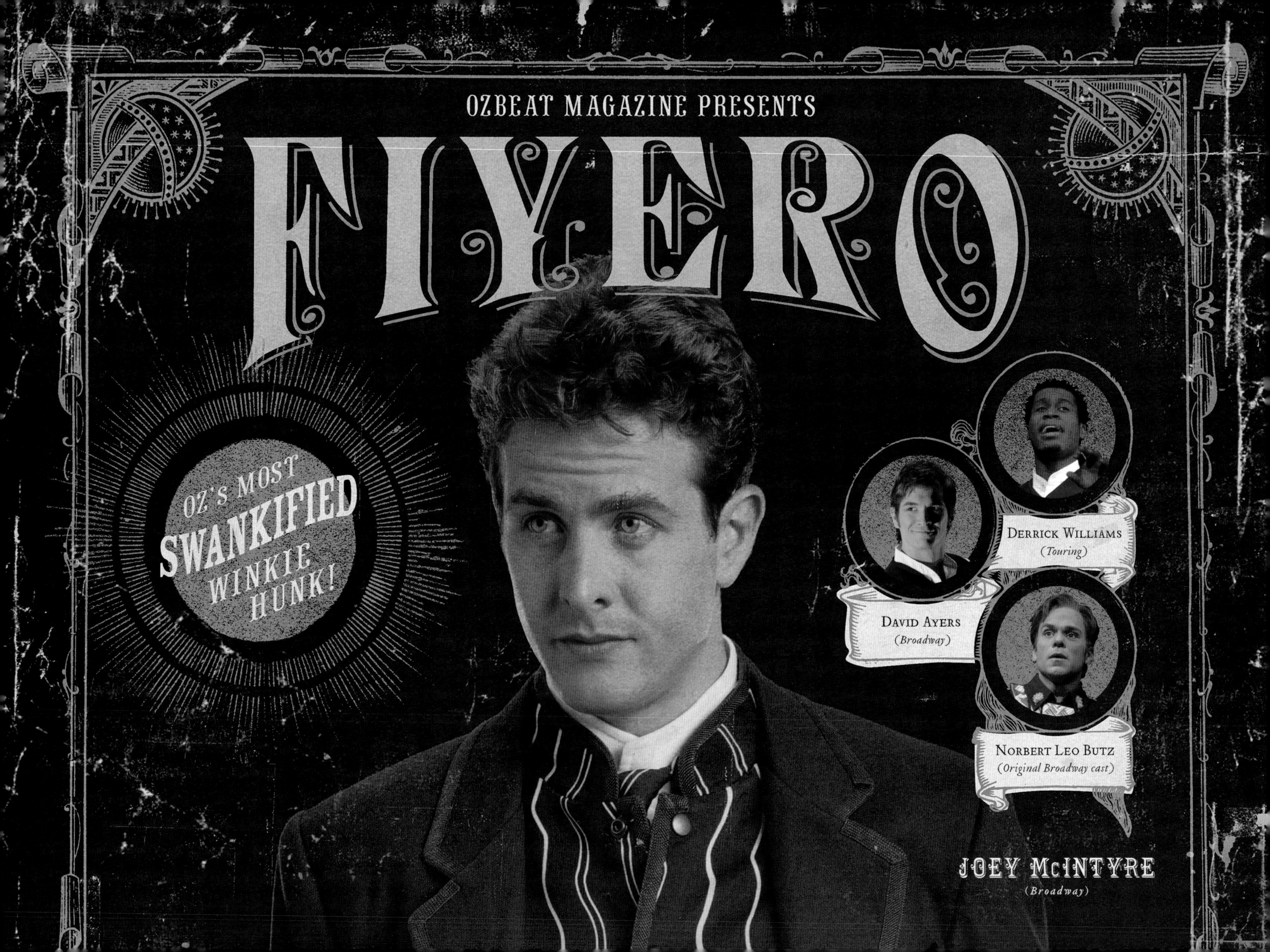

OZBEAT MAGAZINE PRESENTS
FIYERO
OZ'S MOST SWANKIFIED WINKIE HUNK!
DERRICK WILLIAMS
(Touring)
DAVID AYERS
(Broadway)
NORBERT LEO BUTZ
(Original Broadway cast)
JOEY McINTYRE
(Broadway)

All my Love —

Fiyero

xoxoxox

HISTORIOGRAPHICAL HIGHLIGHTS

When he came to Shiz University, Fiyero brought his "scandalacious" reputation for being a pleasure-loving playboy always getting booted out of schools. However, his life is changed by an uneasy friendship with Elphaba, then his reluctant alliance with the Wizard and tentative engagement to Glinda. Ultimately, when it comes to choosing between Glinda and Elphaba, Fiyero gets serious and makes a risky decision.

HAILS FROM WHICH OZ PROVINCE

Winkie Country

FREQUENTLY SEEN WITH

The coolest kids at Shiz, hanging out and not studying. Then, at the Emerald City, with Glinda at public ceremonies. Around the time of the Wicked Witch's melting, he mysteriously disappears.

DEFINISH DEMEANOR

Gorgeous looks and his snappy Winkie Prince uniform

SIGNATURE UTTERANCE

"Excuse me, there's no pretense here: I happen to be genuinely self-absorbed and deeply shallow."

PRIMUS PRINCIPIA PHILOSOPHICA

"Dancing through life, skimming the surface, gliding where turf is smooth. Life's more painless for the brainless; Why think too hard, when it's so soothing dancing through life . . ."

BOQ

HISTORIOGRAPHICAL HIGHLIGHTS

Boq is an unusually tall Munchkin—socially ambitious families married into height. He attends Shiz University, where he falls hopelessly in love with Galinda. Of course, Galinda barely knows he exists. As a favor, Boq escorts Elphaba's wheelchair-bound sister, Nessarose, to the Ozdust Ballroom dance. Nessarose mistakenly thinks Boq is in love with her. When Nessarose becomes the Governor of Munchkinland, she retains Boq as a manservant. His life is utterly changed when Elphaba comes back to visit.

HAILS FROM WHICH OZ PROVINCE
Munchkinland

FREQUENTLY SEEN WITH
Nessarose, as he pines for Galinda

DEFINISH DEMEANOR
Trouble is, Boq is so ordinary,
he gets lost in a crowd.

SIGNATURE UTTERANCE
*"I know I'm just a mere Munchkin.
But even a Munchkin has feelings!"*

PRIMUS PRINCIPIA PHILOSOPHICA

"I lost my heart to Glinda the moment I first saw her."

CHRISTOPHER FITZGERALD

(Original Broadway cast, above.)

NESSAROSE

HISTORIOGRAPHICAL HIGHLIGHTS

Nessarose is the "tragically beautiful" daughter of the Governor of Munchkinland. Because her older sister, Elphaba, was born green, her mother chewed milk flowers to ensure a dermatologically correct second baby. Unfortunately, Nessarose was born with deformed legs. Still, Nessarose is her father's favorite; he gives her beautiful silver slippers when she goes to Shiz. At school, Nessarose becomes convinced that Boq loves her, which, of course, he doesn't. Later in life, when she becomes the cruel and reclusive Governor of Munchkinland, Nessarose crosses paths with her sister, now the Wicked Witch of the West. She learns the power of *The Grimmerie.*

HAILS FROM WHICH OZ PROVINCE
Munchkinland

FREQUENTLY SEEN WITH
Wheelchair and silvery-jeweled slippers

DEFINISH DEMEANOR
Sad eyes, pretty pink dress

SIGNATURE UTTERANCE
"You fly around Oz, trying to rescue Animals you've never even met— and not once have you ever thought to use your power to rescue me."

PRIMUS PRINCIPIA PHILOSOPHICA

"Alone and loveless here, with just the girl in the mirror. Just her and me— the Wicked Witch of the East! We deserve each other . . ."

MICHELLE FEDERER

(Original Broadway cast, above.)

Shiz University

IN OZ WE TRUST

DOCTOR DILLAMOND

and that Beastly Business in Oz

Doctor Dillamond is *Wicked* (the musical)'s main Animal representative and its most passionate civil rights defender. Unlike most of the other Animals represented in the production (an Antelope midwife, a Rat waiter, and Monkey servants), Doctor Dillamond occupies a position of authority as a respected historian at Shiz University. Yet even he falls before the repressive policies of the Wizard, who has convinced Ozians that allowing Animals to talk and enjoy social equality is a national danger. "The best way to bring folks together," the Wizard says ominously, "is to give them a really good enemy." In Gregory Maguire's novel, this political tragedy is elaborated more fully, and the parallel between Animal subjugation in Oz and the reality of human persecution is more pronounced. However, in *Wicked*, the Animal subplot is extremely important; it supplies Elphaba with her motivation to oppose the Wizard and it gives the fantasy world of Oz a gritty and thought-provoking new dimension.

HEADMISTRESS

DEPT. HEAD

№ 020653

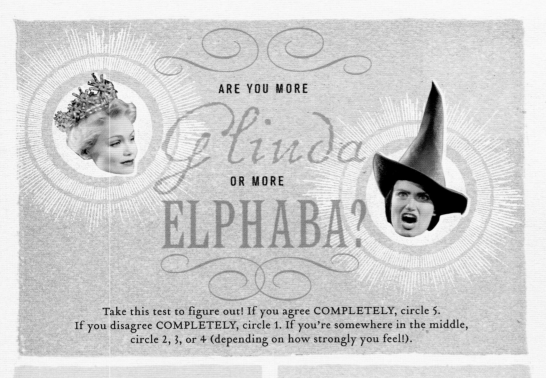

ARE YOU MORE

Glinda

OR MORE

ELPHABA?

Take this test to figure out! If you agree COMPLETELY, circle 5.
If you disagree COMPLETELY, circle 1. If you're somewhere in the middle,
circle 2, 3, or 4 (depending on how strongly you feel!).

GLINDA

You go all glass-is-half-full about pretty much everything.

1 2 3 4 5

Your friends routinely remind you how fantastic you are.

1 2 3 4 5

You get along really, really well with your parents.

1 2 3 4 5

You love to be the center of attention.

1 2 3 4 5

Your brain is always craving more knowledge.

1 2 3 4 5

Your flirtation skills are second to none!

1 2 3 4 5

You're the It Girl on all the party lists.

1 2 3 4 5

A fun weekend activity is a big dance party.

1 2 3 4 5

Your friends would describe you as a social butterfly.

1 2 3 4 5

TOTAL GLINDA POINTS:

9–20 Not That Girl

You're hardly a Glinda; you're quiet and shy and maybe even a bit of a rebel. Glinda might tell you to try to be more popular, but you like just being you!

21–33 Dancing Through Life

You love hanging with your friends and having fun at a dance. But you also have a serious side—reading a good book is sometimes as fun as a party!

34–45 Popular!

Glinda would approve! You are always surrounded by your friends—you're the ultimate party girl! Talking to new people is fun, and you're never in a bad mood.

ELPHABA

You speak your mind, even if it makes you some enemies.

1 2 3 4 5

You'd rather keep your crush a secret.

1 2 3 4 5

You want to change the world.

1 2 3 4 5

Your friends would describe you as a rebel.

1 2 3 4 5

You look excellent in green.

1 2 3 4 5

You sometimes get picked last during gym.

1 2 3 4 5

Your teachers think you're something special.

1 2 3 4 5

A fun weekend activity is a march or a rally.

1 2 3 4 5

Your friends would describe you as passionate and fiery.

1 2 3 4 5

TOTAL ELPHABA POINTS:

9–20 What Is This Feeling?

You're no Elphaba—you're too outgoing for that! Elphaba might like to go it alone, but you like to be with your friends.

21–33 For Good

You like having others around, but you'll part with the crowd and stand up for your beliefs. Sometimes you're quiet, but you always speak your mind!

34–45 Defying Gravity

You march to the beat of your own drum! You're true to yourself, no matter what. Elphaba would approve: You're a true individual!

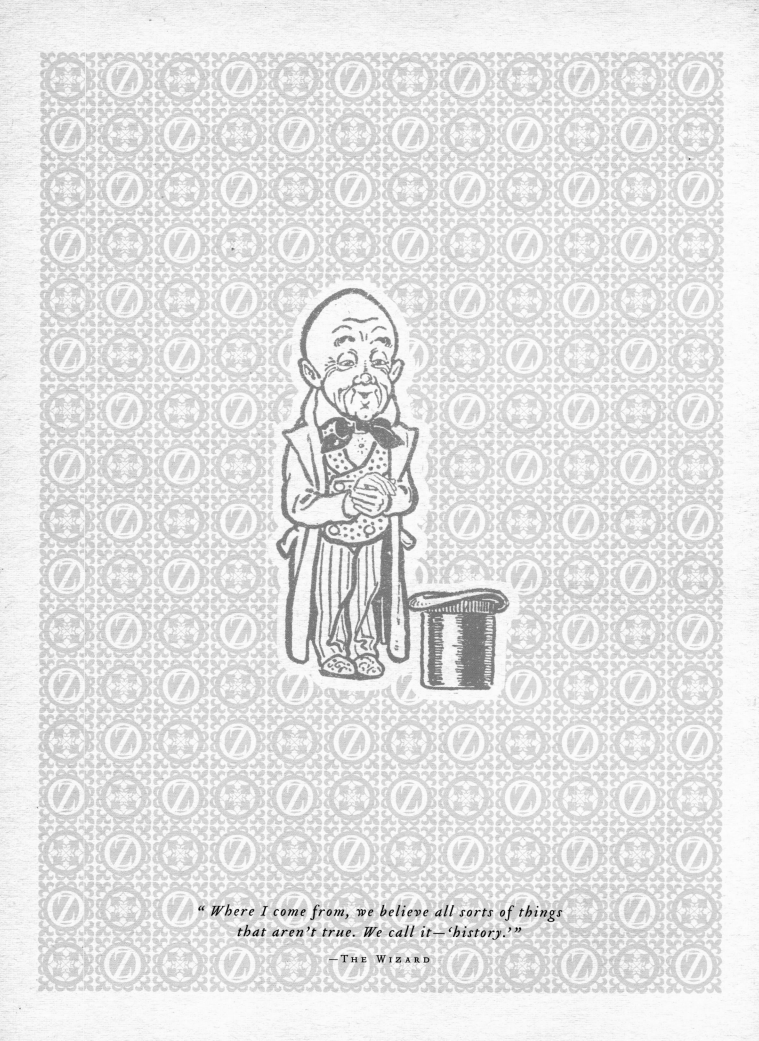

" Where I come from, we believe all sorts of things
that aren't true. We call it—'history.'"

—THE WIZARD

Part Three

FROM PAGE TO STAGE

HERE'S A SAYING IN HOLLYWOOD THAT YOU MAKE THREE MOVIES: THE MOVIE YOU WRITE, THE MOVIE YOU FILM, AND THE MOVIE YOU EDIT. PROBABLY MORE VERSIONS APPLY IN THE MAKING OF A MUSICAL. DIRECTOR JOE MANTELLO HAD A HAND IN STEERING the script of *Wicked* from workshops to its eventual home on Broadway. But even he admitted that when so many cooks are in the kitchen, it's hard to identify who added what spice.

JOE MANTELLO: Once these big shows are finished, everybody has their own version of who was responsible for what, and how it all came to be. Ultimately, the final decisions rest with the director. But there are lots of compromises along the way. I could say to Stephen and Winnie, "In order to get from here to there, we have to cut this section." And they would agree or disagree. The book writing has to be the most accommodating, though, because it is the glue that holds everything together. You might need two extra lines because an actress has to run underneath the stage to make an entrance from a trapdoor.

WINNIE HOLZMAN: Joe was really insightful when it came to telling the story of the Animals in Oz. He helped us see that part of the plot in a whole other way.

JOE MANTELLO: We struggled with the talking-Animal story line for a very long time, even as far as San Francisco, because it was important to the story, but it was more the MacGuffin—the thing that motors the story along. It had to be important enough so that Elphaba could invest in it as a cause and let it politicize her. But it couldn't be so complicated that it would bore the audience. And the book is very dark and political. We were always trying to find the right balance within the plot. That was probably our biggest struggle over the years. If you emphasize it too much, it will start to look ridiculous. Ultimately, we felt that it was really a story of the two girls. When we focused on them, it was successful.

WINNIE HOLZMAN: It didn't occur to me until I had written a few drafts just how few stories there are about women friendships. You have to understand: I didn't sit down and say, "I'm going to write a musical about women friendships." But women were having really strong reactions. Not to discount men who enjoy the piece, but it was almost like women were just starved for stories like these. That came as a surprise. I'd been busy trying to tell the story and figure out the plot, and then one day we kind of looked up and it was like, Wow, this has a strong effect on people.

JOE MANTELLO: And yet we had to move the plot forward. Animals could speak, and they coexisted with humans. In early drafts, Doctor Dillamond was doing all sorts of experiments to prove that animals had souls. There were scenes in his laboratory, and then he was killed under suspicious circumstances. And there was a funeral scene where Galinda changes her name to Glinda. So there was a very tricky balance. We used Gregory's novel as a resource, and the map on the preshow curtain comes directly from the novel. And

DON'T BE SILENCED.
SPEAK OUT BEFORE IT'S TOO LATE!

SOMETHING
BAAAD
IS HAPPENING
IN OZ

with certain set pieces like the Clock of the Time Dragon, we tried to capture what Gregory created, so that people who love the novel wouldn't be disappointed. But Stephen and Winnie don't get enough credit for the plotting of the show—it really is their own construction. Particularly where it meets up with the movie and the way Boq and Fiyero become the Tin Woodsman and the Scarecrow. People who haven't read the novel might think that was Gregory's creation.

STEPHEN SCHWARTZ: Gregory came to a reading in New York about a year or so before the San Francisco tryouts. And I remember being extremely nervous because we had changed so much of his story. His attitude always was, "I wrote the book the way I saw it. And you guys do what you need to do. As long as it stays true to the basic concept and tone, I'll be happy." And he just was supportive the whole way.

GREGORY MAGUIRE: At that December workshop, I was initially sorry about agreeing to do it. I felt that *Wicked* the novel was a tragedy. Elphaba dies fairly young. She's young, she's powerful, she's slightly misguided, but her heart is in the right place. And she dies. And that's what makes a tragedy. It's not quite as tragic when you die old in bed, happy with your family around you. So I gulped a little bit. I did make a couple of proposals to Marc Platt. He asked me for notes, and I provided him with about five pages of them. I'm not sure if they were passed on to anybody, but I did provide them. Nonetheless, once I actually saw *Wicked* onstage and saw how it worked in front of an audience, I found myself making my peace with it very quickly, for a number of reasons. One is that there is still a hugely bittersweet feeling to the ending. And if you think of *Wicked* the musical as the story of the friendship between Glinda and Elphaba, then the fact that they are separated from each other, never to speak again, is almost as good as a death. It's still poignant and dreadful and sad.

"Oh, Miss Elphaba. The things one hears these days. Dreadful things . . ."

—DR. DILLAMOND

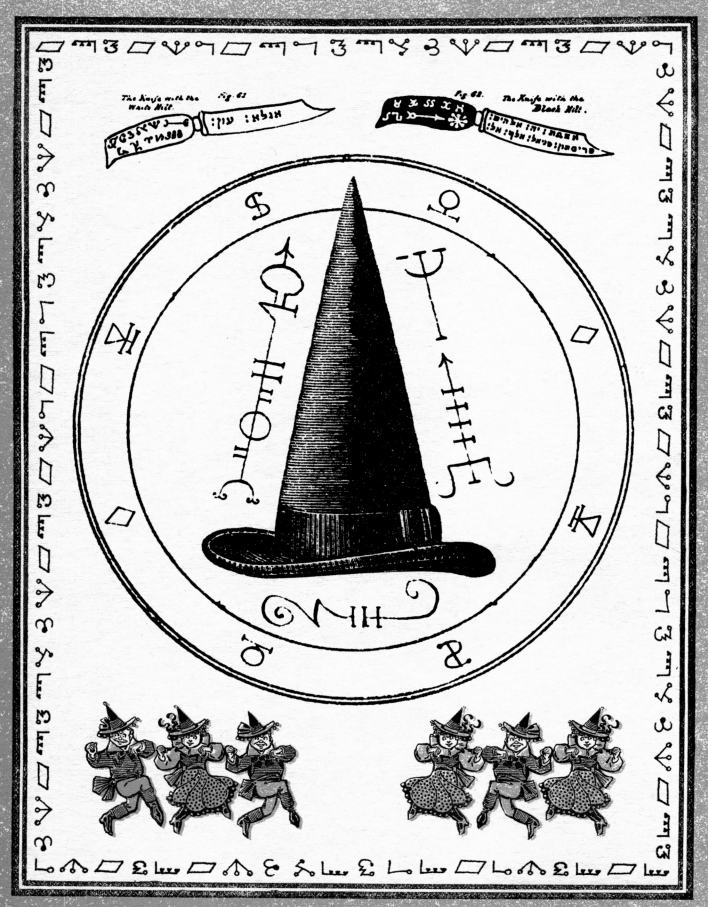

PLATE III.

NOW AT LAST, SHE'S DEAD AND GONE! NOW AT LAST,
THERE'S JOY THROUGHOUT THE LAND

CHAPTER III

DANCING THROUGH LIFE

THE SUMPTUOUS ORCHESTRAL SOUND ONE HEARS IN *WICKED* IS the end product of a long, immensely complicated process of composition, lyric writing, tweaking, and compromise. But each song began the same simple way: with Stephen Schwartz scribbling ideas, titles, rhymes, and snatches of lyrics in his many notebooks, then sitting at a piano in his home in Connecticut, plunking out various melodic lines. *Wicked*'s libretto is composed of two elements: the score, which is the music and lyrics, and Winnie Holzman's "book," or nonmusical scenes. Schwartz, like his contemporary Stephen Sondheim, is an old-fashioned composer-lyricist: He hears the music as he writes the words, and vice versa. To score the world of *Wicked*, it was Schwartz's task to find the perfect style of music as well as the perfect words. But, as he is quick to point out, Holzman, director Joe Mantello, and producer Marc Platt also often contributed to the evolution of a song's style or lyrical content. Here, Schwartz discusses the details of each of his wonderfully wicked songs.

"NO ONE MOURNS THE WICKED"

I HARDLY EVER start by composing the opening number, but this is the song I started writing first. I wanted to open with everyone celebrating, a sort of "Ding Dong the Witch Is Dead" for the Wicked Witch of the West. It's rhythmic and explosive, but somewhat discordant to our ears. To me, it's like music by the modern composer Paul Hindemith. And I have Glinda singing here because Kristin Chenoweth wanted to use her soprano. I had previously thought of Glinda simply as a high belter, as in "Popular." And for a long time, I couldn't figure out how to use her soprano. Then I thought maybe a light little soprano could work for the public Glinda, presenting her face to the world. So Kristin can show from the first minute of the show that she can hit those high A's.

"DEAR OLD SHIZ"

IT'S ALL ABOUT vine-draped walls and ivy-covered statues. I tried to do something that sounded like a school song, with silly lyrics that are slightly archaic. "When grey and sere our hair hath turned / We shall still revere the lessons learned," that sort of thing. I did the vocal arrangement myself—soprano, alto, tenor, bass—a four-part choral harmony. And we recorded it a cappella for the original Broadway cast album.

"THE WIZARD AND I"

IF YOU LOOK at virtually any modern musical—all the way back to Rodgers and Hammerstein—every one has a character come out and sing an "I Want" song. Usually it's the second or third number. And it seems to be a convention in musicals that you defy at your peril! It defines the main character's goal. *Wicked* was structured in such a way that Elphaba had to declare herself. Psychologically, I think it's pretty clear: If you're born green, you're going to feel like an outcast, and most outcasts, on some level, want to become "incasts." No matter how stubbornly proud they are of their outsider status, they yearn to be accepted, valued, and loved. And you have to remember: This is a girl who was shunned not only by society but also by her own family. Then she discovers that her magical talent, which has previously only gotten her into trouble, earns her acceptance from this respected woman, Madame Morrible, who suggests that Elphaba could develop it into something that would get her to the Wizard. And if you're accepted by the Wizard, you're accepted by everybody. It's like becoming the adviser to the president. What I tried to do with the score in general was to find a way to use accessible music that was age-appropriate. Elphaba is young and in college, so she sings something that sounds youthful. I wanted to compose something appropriate for a teenager, but not something about which you could say, "Oh, that sounds like Seattle grunge from the 1990s."

"WHAT IS THIS FEELING?"

THIS WAS THE fifth try for that spot. I would compose a song, and it was more or less the same one. It was always about the first encounter between Glinda and Elphaba, when they are forced to be reluctant roommates and have instant antipathy for each other. The first song I came up with was "Bad Situation," as in, "I have to make the best of a bad situation." (On a side note, early on in the course of writing the show, I had this notion that all the songs would have either the word "good" or "bad" or "wicked" or "better" or something like that in the title. Obviously, I abandoned that. But if you look at the song list, you will see an awful lot of songs with those types of words in their titles.) Winnie gave me the notion of writing a "hate-at-first-sight" song. That seemed like a good idea to me, very amusing. So I listened to a lot of classic falling-in-love songs. And I just wrote down all the phrases from the lyrics. The phrase "What is this feeling" stuck in my head. I set it to a tune that was sort of like "Ten Minutes Ago," the Rodgers and Hammerstein song from *Cinderella*. We all liked the lyrics, but Joe Mantello kept feeling there was something wrong with it. He couldn't put his finger on it. At this point, I was so frustrated that I just thought, Well, I'm staying with this until we get a better idea. Then, as we were going into rehearsal before our San Francisco tryouts, Joe said he had seen *Hairspray*, and he noticed how high energy the first several songs in it were. He called and said, "I think what is bothering me about that song is that it's not high energy enough so early in the show." Of course, he was exactly right. Then I said to him, "OK, I know exactly what to do with this." I went home, and two days later I came in with the song that went into the show.

"SOMETHING BAD"

DURING THE readings in Los Angeles and New York, Winnie and I came to the conclusion that all animals in Oz could speak. Then Marc Platt gave us the idea that, because they're being oppressed and repressed by the Wizard, animals were losing the power of speech—that "something bad" was happening. And to us, that seemed touching and metaphorical. It's also the kind of thing everyone would regret, since we all want animals to speak. Originally, Dr. Dillamond used to bleat a lot throughout. He would be saying, "Miss Elphabaaaa..." and it was sort of a joke. Then Joe had the idea that during the first scene, he shouldn't bleat at all. He should speak very normally and then, as things got worse, it gets harder and harder for him to speak. That evolved into the idea of this song. He would be trying to say "something bad," but it would come out "something baaaaaad" and he'd be horrified by it. It gets a laugh, which we want, but it's also tragic.

"DANCING THROUGH LIFE"

THIS WAS THE last song written for the show. It replaced a number in San Francisco called "Which Way Is the Party?" But the action is the same. Fiyero arrives at Shiz and immediately organizes the students for a dance. Glinda tricks Elphaba into wearing the black pointy hat, and then feels bad about it, and they become friends. But when we cast Norbert Leo Butz as Fiyero, "Which Way Is the Party?" just didn't fit him. Also, I realized in San Francisco that people didn't understand that Fiyero was expressing his philosophy of life. It came off as if we were just trying to do a dance number. So I had to be more overt about stating his philosophy, to party through life. So I came up with "Dancing Through Life." For the music, I had, like, five different new versions, because we couldn't figure out what would work best for Norbert. I did one that sounded like a Frank Sinatra tune; one that was a little bit like "They Can't Take that Away from Me" sung by Fred Astaire; one that was Billy Joel–esque; one that was atonal, but people felt it was too much like Stephen Sondheim; and then I did what I called the "Sting" version. It has a steady bass line, like in "Every Breath You Take." Wayne Cilento, who handled the musical staging for *Wicked*, was instrumental—pardon the pun—in recommending the "Sting" version, because he felt it would lend itself better to the choreography.

"POPULAR"

I USED A bubble-gum sound to try to characterize Glinda's shallowness and teen sensibility. "Popular" is also a little Beatles-esque. I wanted to write something that had no depth whatsoever. It's empty calories. That's who Glinda is at this point. At one time, Winnie had the idea of Glinda trying to dress up Elphaba to look like her. And Marc Platt realized that it was a parallel to *Emma*, the Jane Austen book, or as we used to call it, *Clueless*, because of the Alicia Silverstone movie. So we call this the *Clueless* section of the show, where Glinda, because she's a control freak, decides to transform this girl into somebody like her—which is absurd to do to the Wicked Witch of the West. Then I just tried to write a song that felt like one of those cheerleaders. I knew all these girls in my high school: She was the most popular girl at school, and she always went out with the captain of the football team. She was always the homecoming queen, blond with a little perky nose—the whole thing. And it's a faintly vicious song, because it's really making fun of them. It's meant to be as shallow as possible. And I think that's why people enjoy it, because it's funny in that way. But it's also political. Glinda refers to the fact that politicians and heads of state get by not because they're particularly smart, but because people would like to hang out with them. As for Kristin yodeling on the word popular, I just like yodels, and Kristin is from Oklahoma. So maybe I was thinking unconsciously of country-western music, and I knew she could do it.

"I'M NOT THAT GIRL"

IT'S HARD FOR me to talk about this song. It's funny, because it was one of the easiest ones to write and came pretty early. The situation was so clear: Elphaba is an extremely self-aware person who had a moment when she allowed herself to fall for this handsome guy. And then she has to stop herself from feeling anything, because it was too painful. In a very calm way, she says, "I can't feel that." I decided the song should never get too big. That it should be almost like a music box. It's hard for me to articulate it, because it just came out so fast, but it's the kind of feeling that all of us understand. "Every so often we long to steal / To the land of what might have been / But that doesn't soften the

ache we feel / When reality sets back in." We've all felt it. I certainly have. A moment when you fantasize, and then you realize: Wait a minute. That's not realistic. That's not who I am.

"ONE SHORT DAY"

THIS WAS THE third song I wrote for *Wicked*. I had already done "No One Mourns the Wicked" and "Making Good" (which, in the end, we didn't use). I played them for Marc Platt, and he liked them very much. But I could see that he was a little concerned and, in a very tactful way, he asked me, "Do you think, um, that some of the songs . . ." And I said, "You want to know if there is going to be anything fun in the show, right, Marc?" And he said yes. And I said, "OK, I promise!" Winnie and I had the idea that when Elphaba and Glinda go to the Emerald City, it should be like two girls in Paris for a day. So it's supposed to be a spree, basically: energetic and celebratory. Another thing I wanted to do was have them go to the theater to see *Wizomania*. It's like Mussolini's Italy, where everything is in service of "our great leader." That allowed me to poke fun musically at some old-fashioned musicals that I love, like *Funny Girl* and *Gypsy*.

"A SENTIMENTAL MAN"

HERE THE WIZARD longs to be a father, which is obviously very important to the plot. This number sets things up that are important later on. For example, the Wizard sings that "everyone deserves a chance to fly," and the phrase crops up in the next song. When Elphaba hears that line, it affects her deeply, and she'll repeat it later in a bitter, cynical way in "Defying Gravity." Also, no matter how intentionally manipulative and falsely emotional the music is in "A Sentimental Man," on some level the Wizard does mean it. He really wanted to be a father. He is honestly sentimental, even though he's a villain. And, at the end of *Wicked*, when he realizes that he destroyed his own daughter—it's so devastating to him, he's willing to pack it in and leave Oz.

"DEFYING GRAVITY"

I WANTED A series of simple notes that sounded like strength, coming into your own, feeling the power come up from below, from your feet and spreading up through your body. The song's structure evolved over time, because it was originally just for Elphaba, and then we realized that Glinda should be included. There was a whole other song that they sang to each other, called "I Hope You're Happy," which was a very angry, mocking song. And eventually, that got cut down to just a quick verse in "Defying Gravity." I really like that, at one point, they say to each other bitterly and sarcastically, "Well, I hope you're happy, look how you've screwed up." But when they part, they genuinely say to each other, "I hope you will be happy." And it was also very important that for a moment these women look like they're going to join forces, and then Glinda can't do it. From this point on, they go down different paths. And Glinda is going down the path to becoming Glinda the Good, and Elphaba is going down the path to becoming the Wicked Witch of the West. But there's a moment when it could all have been different. So I wanted the music to be powerful and empowering and thrilling. It took a while to come up with the title. I had created a long list of titles for this. And then I finally thought, Well, the phrase "defying gravity" seems right, because I like the word "defying." It's defiant, but it's also about lifting off from earth.

DEFYING GRAVITY

By

STEPHEN SCHWARTZ

How does a song begin? A faint, enticing melody in the head? A phrase overheard on the street that sends the lyricist's mind racing? There seem to be countless ways for a song to originate. At his home in Connecticut, Stephen Schwartz has accumulated piles of notebooks in which he would jot down rhymes, lines, and titles for the songs in *Wicked*. To compose a song, he will sit at a piano and try out melodic lines and write them by hand onto sheet music. Here we see how his musical spirit soars on paper as he creates the sound of "Defying Gravity."

Defying Gravity

ACT II

"THANK GOODNESS"

ELPHABA IS NOW viewed as a terror to Oz. And of course, Madame Morrible and the press are fanning the flames, stoking fear of Elphaba in order to keep themselves powerful. We see Glinda beloved by all of Oz and getting credit for things she didn't do. At this point, I decided her character needed depth. And so I began to think about what was happening inside her. This should be her moment of triumph. This is where she gets everything she ever wanted. She's acclaimed as a good witch. She has the man she loves. It's an engagement party. And yet, she feels fraudulent inside, empty. She's very unhappy, because none of it feels genuine to her. And she's becoming too self-aware. So she's trying to talk herself into feeling happy, that this is a happy ending. But actually, she's in complete despair. She's on the verge of tears.

"WONDERFUL"

"WONDERFUL" IS deliberate pastiche, musically. It was the only place in the show I actually wanted to sound like a specific place and time in our world: early-20th-century Midwestern America. It's a little bit ragtime and vaudeville. What's really going on in the lyrics, of course, is that the Wizard is intellectually seducing Elphaba, who is exhausted and isolated. He's offering her what she desires in the "The Wizard and I," and he even quotes that music. And Elphaba is enticed by this, that she too could be wonderful and celebrated. This is also the most political song in the show. The Wizard talks about how the truth is a lie agreed upon by society. He describes himself as a mediocrity thrust into prominence. That has contemporary reverberations, I think. He also sings what I think is the philosophical core of the show: "There are precious few at ease / With moral ambiguities / So we act as though they don't exist." In the end, that's what *Wicked* is about. For whatever reason, people need to look at things in black and white, to label one person a villain and another a hero.

"I'M NOT THAT GIRL (REPRISE)"

WHEN ELPHABA sings, "I'm Not That Girl" in Act I about Glinda, it's understandable. And then here, suddenly, it turns around, and Glinda sings it about Elphaba. You never see this coming. So that's very neat. And then it segues into the love song between Elphaba and Fiyero, which was enormously satisfying to me.

"AS LONG AS YOU'RE MINE"

IT'S A LOVE song, and it's supposed to sound sexy and passionate. But there's a darkness underneath it, because Elphaba and Fiyero know, even as they sing, that this can't last. They understand that they're fugitives and this is just a moment in time. Hence the title, with another reference to time. By the way, this is one of the scenes that Joe Mantello staged most beautifully. Originally in our script, and in earlier outlines, it was set in a little rented room. And Joe wanted to get it into a more open and mysterious place, so he put it in the forest with a campfire and a lantern and stuff. I think it looks so beautiful, and it's so incredibly romantic.

"NO GOOD DEED"

THIS NUMBER is a bit of me showing off! The piano line is Rachmaninoff-y, very fast, and harmonically complex. And "No good deed goes unpunished" is one of my favorite sayings in the world—I think it's so true. It appeals to the bitter and cynical side of me. Once a month, at least something happens in life when a friend or I will say, "Well, here's another example that no good deed goes unpunished." This is the most operatic moment in the show. It's structured like an opera aria, if you think about it. It has huge range, and it gives Elphaba a lot of vocal pyrotechnics, where she'll hit a big note with "Fiyero!" and then suddenly get soft, and there are places where she sings "Nessa" and "Dr. Dillamond" with the orchestra just sawing away on the violins. Musically, this is the most ambitious thing in the show. And pretty exciting to me.

"MARCH OF THE WITCH HUNTERS"

IT HAS THE same tune as "No Good Deed" but is sung by a mob of angry villagers out of control. This is when you see Elphaba starting to reap what she has sown.

Two good deeds that she has done are viewed—by the people for whom she did them—negatively. She saved the Tin Woodman's life, and he blames her for turning him into tin. She saved the lion cub, and he blames her for the fact that he has no courage. "No Good Deed" and this song are really one whole piece.

"FOR GOOD"

I AVOIDED THIS song for a while, because I knew it was the heart of the show. If we got the final song between the two women right, then we had the show. When I felt ready to do it, I called Winnie, and we had a long brainstorming conversation. I was in Connecticut, and she was in California. We were talking about the content of the song, and I scribbled down a lot of ideas. Winnie was free-associating. At one point, she used the phrase "for good." She said, "You know, they've been in each other's lives, and they've basically changed each other for good." As soon as I heard the phrase, I just said, "OK, stop. I know what to do." It's one of the best titles, and it came out of Winnie's mouth. I love phrases that mean more than one thing. Obviously, the phrase "for good" is a double entendre: It means both "forever" and "for good as opposed to bad." Then I talked to my daughter, Jessica, who is now in her twenties. She has a friend who lives across the country from her but whom

she has known since they were little girls. I said to her, "If you knew that you were never going to see Sarah again, and you had one chance to say goodbye to her and tell her what she has meant in your life, what would you say?" She just started to talk, and I scribbled things down. Pretty much the entire first verse of "For Good" is what she said: People come into our lives for a reason, there are things we learn from each other, and we help each other to grow.

"FINALE"

HERE, WE RETURN to our themes. We're back to the music from "No One Mourns the Wicked." But now, there is something mournful and beautiful about it— we have a completely different response. At the beginning, we took it at face value: The Witch was bad. She is dead. We're glad. And no one is sorry. Now we realize how complicated and multifaceted her story was. And then I bring back a few lines from "For Good" and weave the two themes together. But the villagers don't know Elphaba's story; they accept the myth of the Wicked Witch of the West, the same way the audience accepted it when they entered the theater. The mob is still screaming away—joyfully but discordantly—how Elphaba was "Wicked! Wicked! Wicked!"

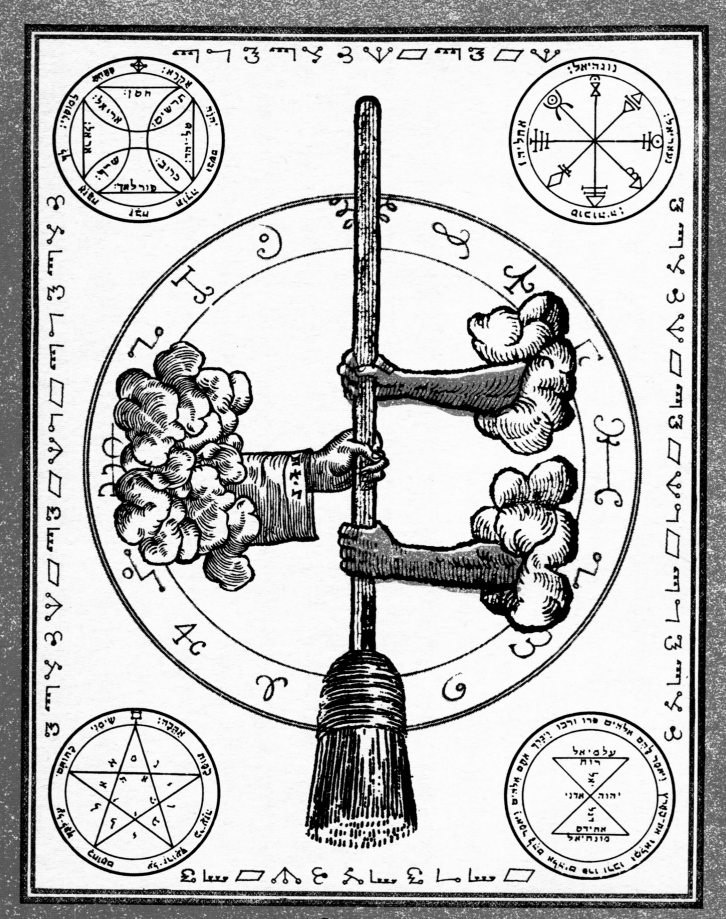

PLATE IV.

As someone told me lately: "Ev'ryone deserves the chance to fly!"

CHAPTER IV

DEFYING GRAVITY

AT THE LAST REHEARSAL BEFORE THE NATIONAL TOUR OF
Wicked ships out to Toronto, actors in sweatpants and T-shirts stretch in a rehearsal room, on a floor
that is marked up with tape to demarcate set pieces. A forest of props and costumes ring the playing
space. Players in the small rehearsal band (drums, percussion, keyboard) hang out, chatting and prac-
ticing their instruments. At a desk, the stage manager scrolls through the hundreds of light and sound
cues on his laptop. A dance captain walks the actors through a couple of routines, making last-minute
tweaks to a scene. Director Joe Mantello sits in the back of the room, taking it all in and whispering
notes to his assistant. The average audience member may be wowed by the "theater magic" on display
in the finished product, but for those who work behind the scenes on a major Broadway show, it's a
business and an industry. In fact, the creation of a Broadway musical, no matter how few people get
the credit or reap the awards, can be a bit like a factory assembly line. Different people are responsible for lights, sound, costumes, dance, special effects, makeup, and dozens of other production effects.

Hundreds of people are needed to create the work in rehearsals, and hundreds more are required to keep the show running on a weekly basis. This mammoth enterprise employs workers at every level: from the stagehand who dumps dry ice into the fog-making machine below the *Wicked* stage, to the Tony Award–winning costume designer who sketched every hat and dress in the show. If the design and technical side of *Wicked* is like a finely tuned machine, here are the master engineers, talking about how they created the visual and aural landscape of the show. Bringing it all together to form one cohesive vision is the director, Joe Mantello.

Part One

READY, SET, GO!

O CREATE THE PHYSICAL WORLD OF *WICKED*, SET DESIGNER EUGENE LEE HAD HIS WORK CUT OUT FOR HIM. WINNIE HOLZMAN'S BOOK TAKES THE CHARACTERS THROUGH TIME AND SPACE, FROM THE IVY-COVERED HALLS OF ACADEME AT SHIZ UNIVERSITY TO THE OPULENT

eye-popping Emerald City, to the wilderness of the Great Gillikin Forest and the play's final scenes at Kiamo Ko, the castle in Winkie County. There are outdoor and indoor scenes that shift in the blink of an eye. All of this has to happen in real time, with seamless transitions between scenes. Luckily, Lee was no stranger to problem solving in set design. For his Tony Award–winning design of 1979's *Sweeney Todd*, he created a movable Victorian chamber of horrors, in which actors wheeled set pieces around the stage. The effect was both practical and Brechtian, i.e., calling attention to its own theatricality. For *Vanya on 42nd Street* (1994), a filmed record of Andre Gregory's production of the Chekhov classic *Uncle Vanya*, Lee made use of the then-dilapidated New Amsterdam Theatre (it would later be renovated and be rechristened by *The Lion King*), using its ruined interior to comment on the characters' inner turmoil. But the unifying image for Lee's set design is inspired by an image in Gregory Maguire's novel: The proscenium is ringed with large, fantastical cogs and gears from an ancient-looking clock, and they're choked with crawling vines. It looks as though Lee were revealing the intricate clockwork of his own craft. In fact, Lee's designs reveal a mind that prefers to peer into the inner workings of stage machinery rather than create a surface illusion.

EUGENE LEE (*Set Designer*): My wife had read the book. And she told me, "If the show is half as good as the book, you really should do it." So I got a copy of the script, which of course would change a lot. I have a little studio in my carriage house in Providence, Rhode Island, and at that time I had a student from Carnegie Mellon helping me. So he and I sat down one weekend and built a big model. I dragged the model to the lobby of the Minetta Lane Theatre in New York for a meeting with Joe Mantello. Joe got the whole show: I sat him in front of the model and I said, "Now, look, just disregard that I'm directing here." I went through the whole show, and he sat there with his head in his hands. And afterward, he said, "Wow, I don't quite see it like that, but this is pretty good." So that was that. Then the writers and the producers wanted to see it. I dragged the model up to their office and did my little show for them, and they hired me. It's hard to judge, but I would say a good 75 percent of what was in that model ended up in the show in some form.

Influences on the set came from everywhere: from W. W. Denslow's illustrations in the Baum books and from the original novel, but not from the movie so much. The main idea of the set is that you're looking at the interior of a giant clock: gears and other mechanisms. By the way, Gregory Maguire should get the credit for that, not me. In his novel, he goes into great detail describing the Clock of the Time Dragon. It's a kind of medieval pageant wagon with small doors and prosceniums, pushed around by dwarves and clowns. Although they don't go into this in the show, the Clock of the Time Dragon is part of a kind of heretical religion in Maguire's version of Oz. I really got into that, because stage mechanics always made me a little nervous: seeing something slide out onstage on its own.

Photographed by Constance Brown, for the New Yorker, January 5, 1998.

Eugene and Henry in the Studio.

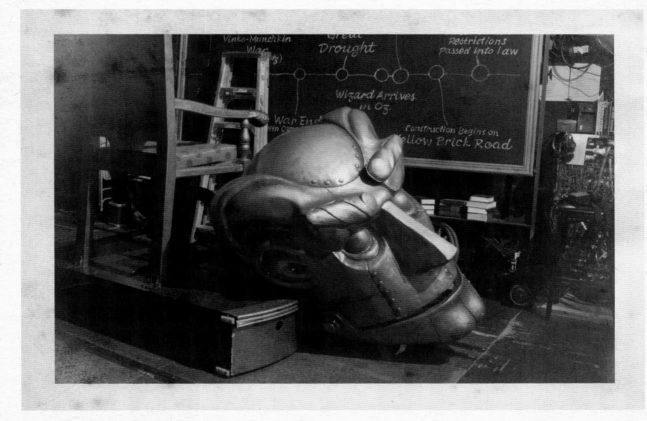

{Top} EUGENE LEE

{Below} *The Wizard's imposing metal head rests between scenes. Lee explains that he found inspiration from a variety of sources, including original Baum illustrator W. W. Denslow.*

Since the 1960s, I've worked at the Trinity Repertory Company in Providence, Rhode Island. We don't have as much money as they do on Broadway, so we have to do things simply. And although *Wicked* had a big budget, there were restrictions—and good ones, in a certain sense. At first, they didn't want the dragon. They really fought the dragon over the proscenium. Of course, it turned out to be the most fun and cheapest thing we did in the whole show. I had help from Bob Flanagan, who is a puppeteer I've used for a long time on *Saturday Night*

stories, these things get embellished over time. But I think it was Joe who had the thought of actually using bubbles. And it was my idea that the giant bubble should look like a mechanical conveyance. And to keep the clock concept, it ended up resembling a pendulum from a clock.

The hardest part of any musical is creating transitions from scene to scene. The script of *Wicked* required

INFLUENCES ON THE SET CAME FROM EVERYWHERE: FROM W. W. DENSLOW'S ILLUSTRATIONS IN THE BAUM BOOKS AND FROM THE ORIGINAL NOVEL, BUT NOT FROM THE MOVIE SO MUCH.

—EUGENE LEE

Live for special props. [Lee is also *SNL*'s production designer.] The first thing I did was call Bob and ask, "Can you make me a puppet dragon that's simple and has ropes on it?"

As for Glinda's bubble machine, I'm not actually sure where that came from. It was probably a combination of things. Like old *Saturday Night Live*

a lot of cutting: You're in a class; you're in a student's room; then you jump to a train station. So I wanted to deal with the space as simply as possible. It's a very simple design at heart. And another thing about it, it's painted all very dark, and it's one of those sets where if the lighting designer doesn't light it right, you won't see it.

{OPPOSITE, TOP} *Susan Hilferty's Flatheads wow the crowds in* Wizomania, *the show-within-a-show that Elphaba and Glinda catch while in the Emerald City. The look of these strange creatures was inspired by the Hammerheads in Baum's first Oz book, which was illustrated by W. W. Denslow.*

{OPPOSITE, BOTTOM} *Eugene Lee combines wood, bicycle mechanics, and the illusion of a horse to create Fiyero's visually witty horse carriage, inspired by Baum and the illustrations by John R. Neill.*

{ABOVE} *Eugene Lee's scale models for the set of* Wicked *prominently feature a mechanical Dragon that looms over the action, as well as plenty of cogs and gears to give a sense of clockwork.*

BEHIND
the
CURTAIN

The WONDROUS and ENCHANTING SETS and PROPS of

EUGENE LEE

Tony Award–winning designer Eugene Lee professes a distrust of illusion, such as the multimillion-dollar spectacles on Broadway, in which huge set pieces effortlessly glide onto stage at the push of a button. That hasn't stopped the master builder from utilizing the most advanced computer technology to create what could almost be called an anti-set—a deconstructed clock environment that displays its gears and workings even as the eye is dazzled by the shifting scenes from a dormitory room at Shiz, to a classroom, to the Wizard's palace in the Emerald City. Set design, Lee likes to say, is all about the transitions.

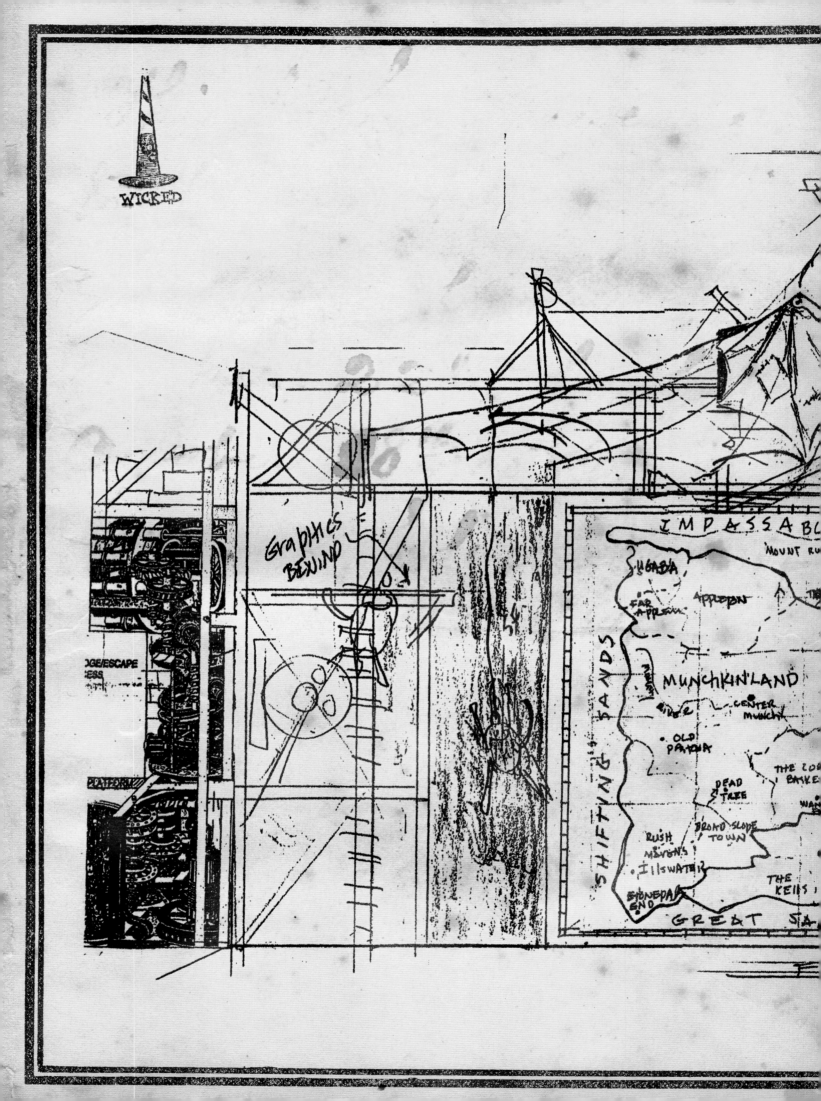

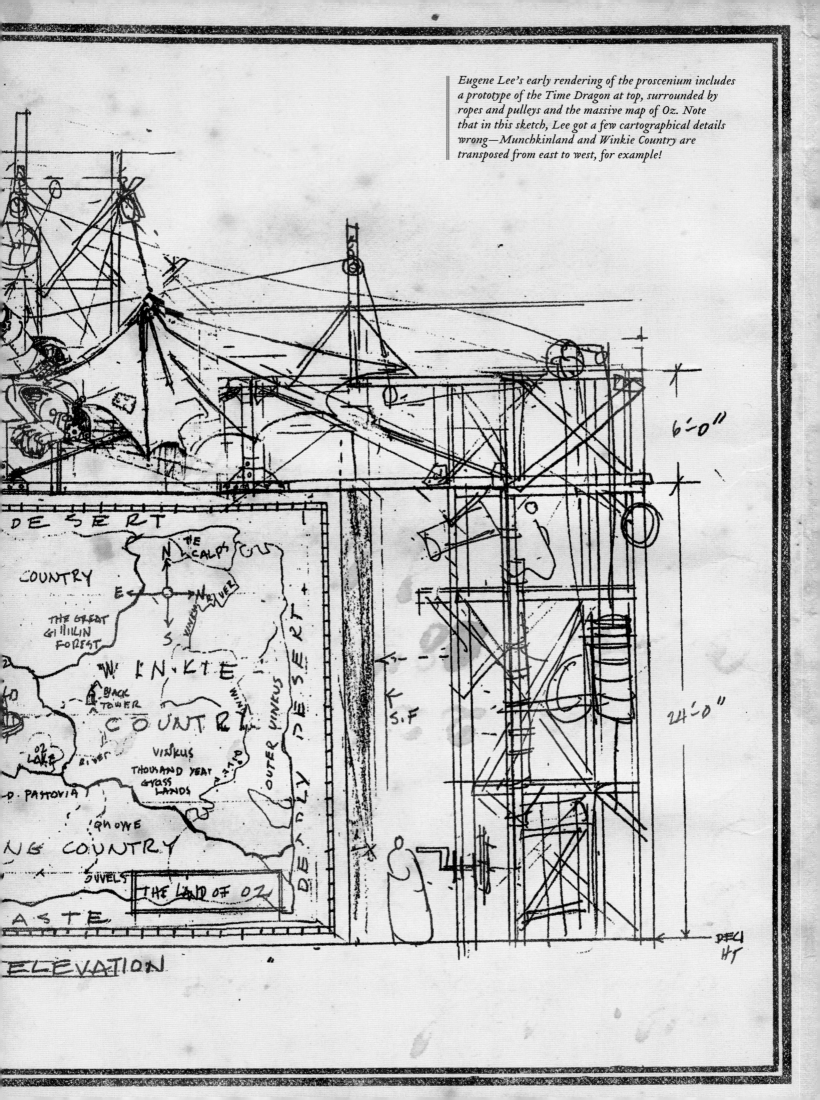

Eugene Lee's early rendering of the proscenium includes a prototype of the Time Dragon at top, surrounded by ropes and pulleys and the massive map of Oz. Note that in this sketch, Lee got a few cartographical details wrong—Munchkinland and Winkie Country are transposed from east to west, for example!

DESERT

COUNTRY

THE GREAT
GI̵I̵I̵I̵I̵N
FOREST

THE CALPS

W I N K I E

BLACK
TOWER

C O U N T R Y

OZ
LAKE

RIVER

VINKUS

THOUSAND YEAR
GRASS
LANDS

OUTER VINKUS

DEADLY DESERT

D. PASTOVIA

QHOWE

NG COUNTRY

5 UVELS

THE LAND OF OZ

ASTE

ELEVATION

6'-0"

24'-0"

S.F

The pre-show curtain displays the magnificent map, which includes Wicked's main locales—Shiz University, the Emerald City, and the Great Gillikin Forest—but also place names that hearken back to other Oz books, such as the Forest of Fighting Trees, Quadling Country, and the Impassable Desert in the south.

FRONT ELEVATION ½"=1'0"

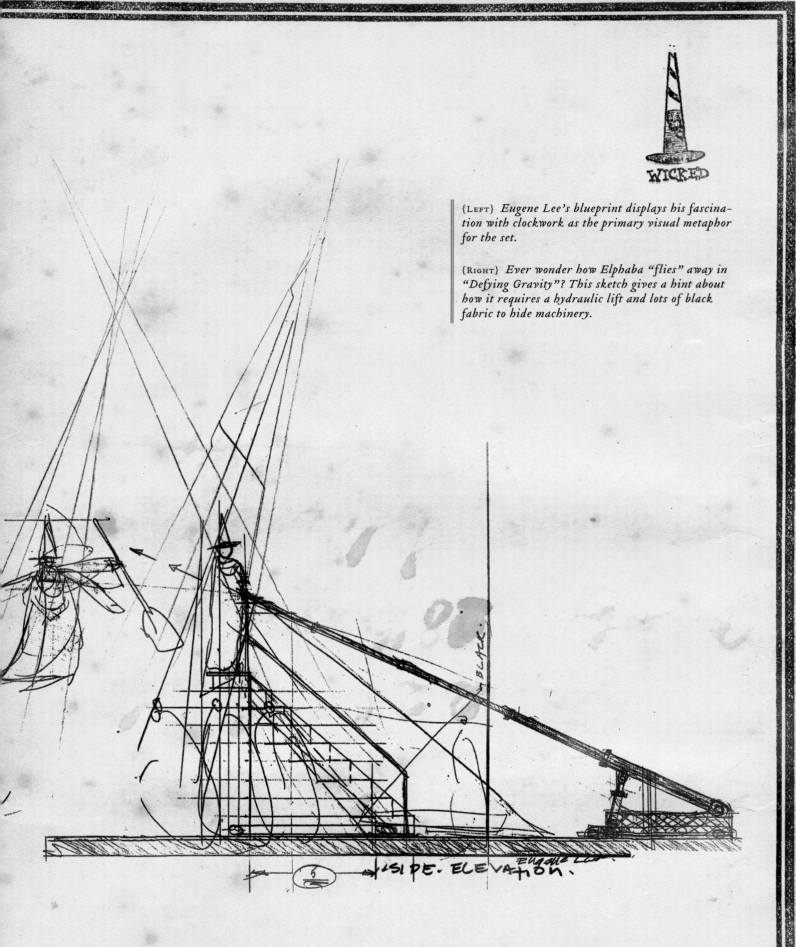

WICKED

{Left} *Eugene Lee's blueprint displays his fascination with clockwork as the primary visual metaphor for the set.*

{Right} *Ever wonder how Elphaba "flies" away in "Defying Gravity"? This sketch gives a hint about how it requires a hydraulic lift and lots of black fabric to hide machinery.*

BLACK

SIDE ELEVATION

Eugene Lee

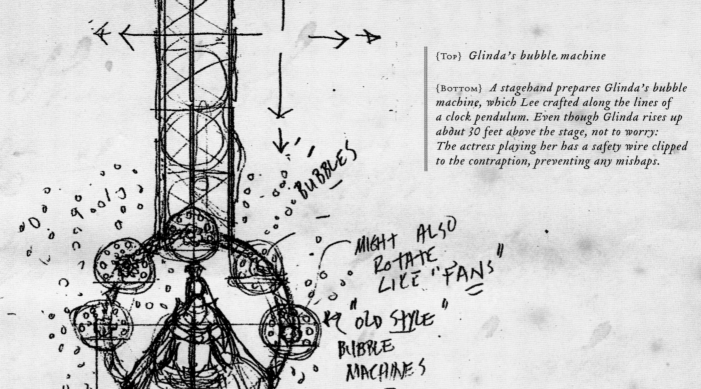

BUBBLES

MIGHT ALSO ROTATE LIKE "FANS"

R "OLD STYLE" BUBBLE MACHINES

{TOP} *Glinda's bubble machine*

{BOTTOM} *A stagehand prepares Glinda's bubble machine, which Lee crafted along the lines of a clock pendulum. Even though Glinda rises up about 30 feet above the stage, not to worry: The actress playing her has a safety wire clipped to the contraption, preventing any mishaps.*

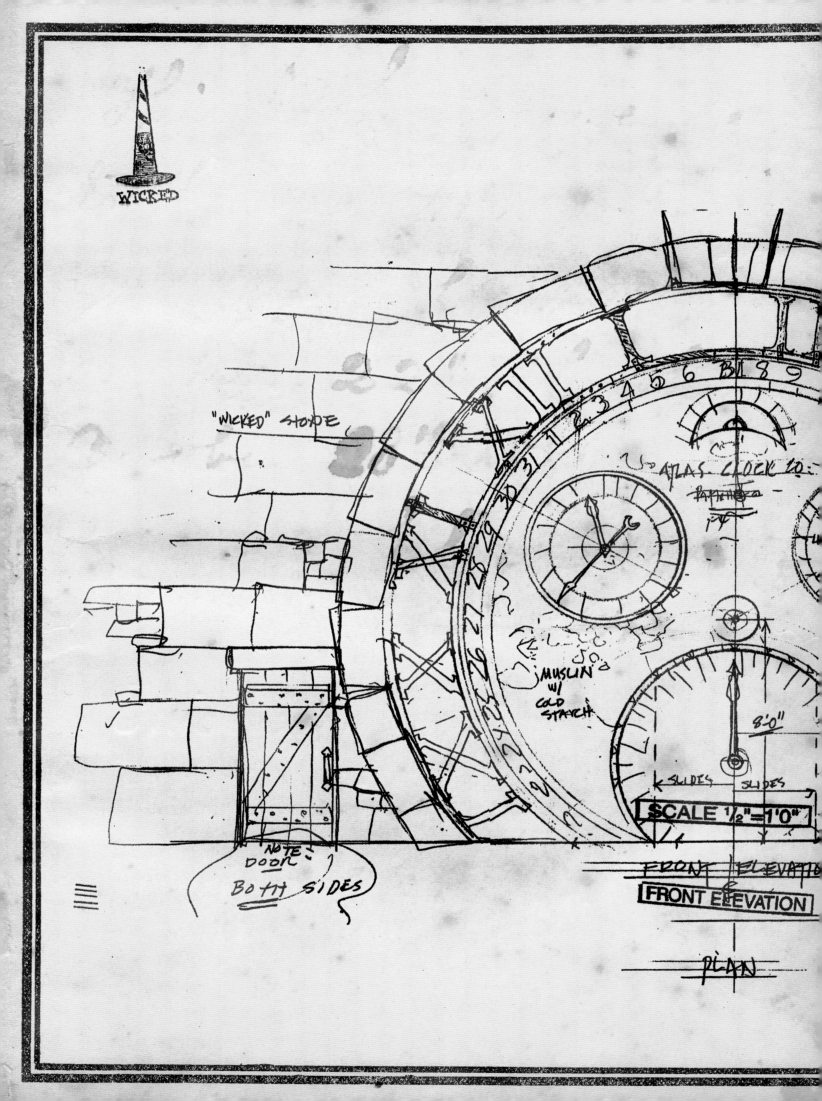

CAST IRON
BOLTS, RIVOTS 'ETC'

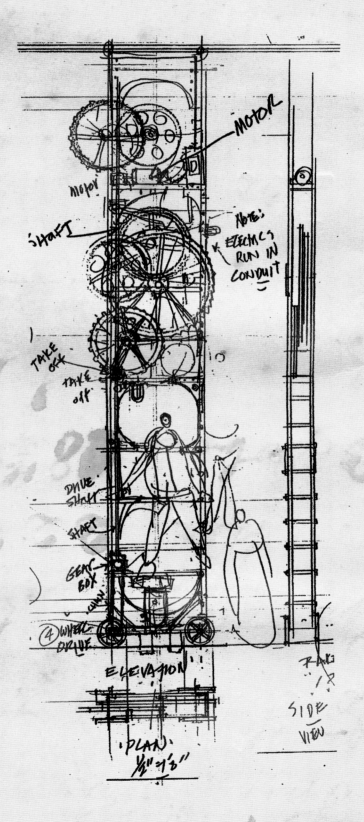

Here, Eugene Lee's sketch shows the giant clock face that serves as the background for the opening and closing scenes of Wicked. Note Lee's notes to the set builders: "Cast iron—bolts, rivets, etc." The sketch at right also shows how Lee's "towers" are not only visually intriguing, but useful. His notes indicate that the light tower is moveable and incorporates a "motor" and "gear box."

FACE

2'0

NOTE
20'0" or

Eugene Lee

MOTOR

motor

SHAFT

NOTE:
ELECTRICS
RUN IN
CONDUIT

TAKE
OFF

TAKE
off

DRIVE
SHAFT

SHAFT

GEAR
BOX

4 WHEEL
DRIVE

ELEVATION

PLAN
½" = 1'8"

RAKE
18"

SIDE
VIEW

Talk about an odd couple! Here's Elphaba and Galinda's dormitory room at Shiz. Note how austere and severe Elphaba's bed (left) is; all she has is a book on her shelves. Galinda has a much frillier, fluffier bed and about 24 pairs of shoes.

THE WIZARD HEAD, FRONT VIEW

Even if you know that his "magic" is a matter of lights and spurting fog, the Wizard head in action is no less scary.

THE WIZARD HEAD, REAR VIEW

The rear view of the Wizard head tells a different story altogether. Look closely and you can see the earthly bric-a-brac that goes into the Wizard's technology: a clock {bottom left}, a movie projector {bottom center}, and even a Sousaphone {upper right}, in addition to a maze of tubes, lights, and wires.

❧ NESSAROSE'S WHEELCHAIR, ACT I ❧

Nessarose's Act I wheelchair as designed by Lee is simple and functional, with a look that evokes Edwardian-era conveyances.

❧ NESSAROSE'S WHEELCHAIR, ACT II ☙

When Nessarose becomes Governor of Munchkinland, she upgrades her wheelchair with inlaid gold and plush red velvet upholstery.

∿⊱ GALINDA'S LUGGAGE ⊰∿

For her first appearance at Shiz University, Galinda brings enough luggage to last all four terms! In Eugene Lee's design,
notice the visual double-entendre of having a G included on the suitcase design. Gucci or Galinda?

❦ ELPHABA'S BROOM ❧

For the climactic Act I finale, "Defying Gravity," Elphaba enchants a broomstick as her escape from the Wizard's palace.
Special effects designer Chic Silber created the illusion in a surprisingly simple fashion: The broomstick is basically raised in the air on a stick
through a trapdoor, and Elphaba lifts it away. The trick is helped by Silber's generous use of dry ice–generated fog.

TWO TECHNICIANS BACKSTAGE HELP THE WIZARD GET HIS HEAD TOGETHER.

In addition to its visual impact as a puppet, the Wizard head features built-in mechanisms that set off clicking mechanical sound effects.

Part Two

AUDIO VISUAL

THE SOUND AND LIGHT DESIGN FOR *WICKED* IS LIKE MAGIC: A MATTER OF SMOKE AND MIRRORS. THEY SEDUCE THE EYE AND EAR WHILE MASKING STAGE MACHINERY OR FOOLING YOU WITH STAGE TRICKS. FOR LIGHTING DESIGNER KENNETH POSNER AND SOUND DESIGNER TONY MEOLA,

the challenges for *Wicked* were manifold: filling the vast Gershwin Theatre with enough light changes to keep the eye engaged; distinguishing the voices of the cast through a sound mixer and adding in sound effects. Posner's lights help define space in each scene, using an astounding 800 individual units, some of which can reposition and mix colors at the push of a computer button. In terms of sound, Meola had to arrange his speakers around Lee's idiosyncratic set and find ways to balance softness and loudness, so that every lyric can be heard distinctly. In both cases, sound and light were used both to enhance a scene and provide cover for what was going on "behind the curtain."

KENNETH POSNER (*Lighting Designer*): It's funny: I built a career on making people not look green onstage. And then all of a sudden, I have to balance a light-costumed pink girl against a dark-costumed green girl! Very challenging. But I collaborated very closely with Joe Dulude, who did the makeup, to discover the exact shade of green to use for Elphaba's lights. She always has a green light on her, by the way, to accentuate the makeup.

To me, lighting is storytelling. There are about 54 scenes and locations in the show, and I have to give each one its distinct light and mood. In terms of the most challenging scene to light, that would be Emerald City. I had to balance the green of the environment with the

green in Susan Hilferty's costumes but still allow you to see the people and the actors. It's also the biggest production number in the play, so the lights are constantly changing and moving, to underscore Glinda and Elphaba's travel through the city. It's such an epic story that we're telling, I'm really proud of the overall design. But if I had to pick a favorite section, I'm really fond of the way the Emerald City looks.

Adinah Alexander operates the Wizard head using a device that resembles bicycle handles and foot pedals, which moves the head but also sets off special sound effects. Meanwhile, the Wizard—George Hearn—waits for his cue at right.

‡ 115 ‡

In "Defying Gravity," the challenge is to actually give the illusion of Elphaba flying. It's done by using green fractured crystals behind her in a very abstract way and making her body float in the middle of the space. Again, the lights underscore the power of the number. The light has a lot of "attack" in the final moment of Act I, meaning intensity. At the peak of the number, right before we go to blackout, it achieves maximum visual impact. Hopefully, it's one of the elements that contribute to the "goose bumps" factor.

TONY MEOLA (*Sound Designer*): My job is to do two things: design the sound for the show and then design the sound for the theater in which it plays. The Gershwin Theatre in New York is a difficult sound house. It's so big, and I really think that as time marches forward, acousticians and architects learn less about sound in the theater than they did a long

time ago. Ninety-five percent of what I do has nothing to do with equipment. If you have a singer onstage but can't hear her because the band is too loud, there could be several reasons. The musical director may have the orchestra playing too loud; the director may place the performer upstage, so we don't hear her voice so well; the choreographer might have had the performer dancing too much before she sang. There are so many things you have to look into. If you just turn up the volume, you get into trouble. It's the difference between pianissimo and fortissimo in a show that makes it exciting.

One of my problems was the Clock of the Time Dragon being smack dab in the middle of the proscenium where I usually put a speaker cluster. So I had to split my speaker cluster left and right of the Dragon. I also hid more speakers along the sides of the stage, where all the vines are.

Idina Menzel glows with witchy energy in "Defying Gravity," thanks to Kenneth Posner's evocative green-hued lights.

There's an actor who manipulates the Wizard head. She stands behind the head with a device that looks like bicycle handlebars with pull breaks and a foot pedal with a kick-drum. These three devices activate different things in the Wizard head: the jaw opening and closing, the eyebrows lifting and dropping, and the eyes swiveling. What I did was attach little switches onto each of the devices, so each has a sound. When the eyebrows go up and down, there's a "click-clunk" sound, for example.

The most sonically dense part of the show is the end of Act I, "Defying Gravity." Elphaba's up in the air, singing her lungs out, "Nothing's gonna bring me down," while the chorus is also singing, "Look at her, she's wicked. Get her!" Glinda is also singing there, and of course you have the full orchestra. It is difficult to juggle all that so it's not screaming loud, but you can still hear everybody.

We recorded lots of special sound effects for the show. There were a lot more animal sounds in the show. Unfortunately, most of them were cut by the time we got to New York. But of course we still have the flying monkey sounds. We created those by recording creaking wood. When I saw Eugene's set, with all that wood, I started playing around with different types of wood: creaking, crunching, twisting it. Taking balsa wood and crunching in your fist in front of a microphone, or stepping on it. It's amazing the sounds you can create to represent a thing that look nothing like the thing itself.

Shadow and silhouette are as powerful as brightness, as demonstrated by the way Posner lights Dorothy's fallen farmhouse, cantilevered within a cornfield.

Part Three

DRESS FOR SUCCESS

ESIDES THE SET AND LIGHTS AND SOUND, MUCH OF THE "HEAVY LIFT-ING" OF THE NARRATIVE FOR *WICKED* IS DONE BY THE COSTUMES. MORE THAN 200 COSTUMES, EACH INDIVIDUALLY TAILORED FOR THE PARTIC-ULAR ACTOR, SPRANG FROM THE FERTILE MIND OF SUSAN HILFERTY, not to mention double that number in shoes and hats, each with a unique, eccentric design. With a resumé that boasts work on more than 200 stage productions that span Broadway, opera, and experimental theater, Hilferty had a unique assignment with *Wicked*: to create from whole cloth a believable world of Winkies, Munchkins, and those iconic witches. Being the chair of the Department of Design for Stage and Film at NYU's Tisch School of the Arts, Hilferty put on her academic cap to work out the puzzle of Oz.

SUSAN HILFERTY (*Costume Designer*): In many ways, I consider myself a historian, a sociologist, and an art historian—in addition to all the other things that I do with clothes. To me, what was so exciting about *Wicked* was trying to understand a world that had a con-nection to the turn of the century as we know it. But I also had to incorporate the idea that animals talk, that there is magic, and that there are Munchkins in this place called Oz. So the design process meant researching history and creating a parallel universe. My research focused on the period in which Baum wrote the books, from 1900 to about 1920. So in a way, it's centered on the Wizard, who is our representative in Oz. The Wizard is somebody from 1900 who has gone up in a balloon and somehow drifted over to Oz. So I created a style I call "twisted Edwardian." It's Edwardian-era suits and dresses, but asymmetrical—the collar might be off cen-ter, or the cut of the dress twists around crazily.

For the student uniforms at Shiz University, I played with things that you recognize in school uni-forms, but I put them together in different ways. Somebody has one type of shirt, or their tie is out, or they're wearing a crazy sweater with one arm in a sleeve and the other bare, men in skirts. It was all to get a "Shiz look." Basically, I came up with the idea of a Shiz school store, where you can mix and match dif-ferent tops and bottoms to suit your personality, even though everything still has the same Shiz pattern of blue and white stripes. That's really at the heart of the play: the struggle between individuality and uniformity. It's also a fashion issue in general. People think they're renegades, but they're actually just following a trend. Back in the '50s, leather jackets became a symbol of rebellion because bikers wore them. Now, of course, it's a fashion thing. That's why, for me, it's interesting to have Elphaba be in her school uniform when she goes to the party during "Dancing Through Life." She's got the hat, she's got her big old boots on, and somehow she doesn't have the "fashion gene." And the other stu-dents are really about, "Oh, we know how to put it all together, and you missed it." But there's nothing so horrific about her when she enters the Ozdust Ball-room, other than not following the fashion rules.

Of the whole show, the costumes in the Emerald City were the easiest thing to do, because it's just no-holds-barred, delirious dressmaking. It's like an imag-inary runway show, and I could be twenty different designers in the Emerald City. One element I wanted to

Madame Morrible's costumes get more and more elaborate throughout the show. The character is played here by Carole Shelley.

work in—besides all the different shades of green, the extravagant hats, and more of the twisted Edwardian formal wear—was the use of animals. If you look closely, many of the costumes have fur and feathers. Thematically, I thought it was important to show how people in the Emerald City, who have money and live the high life, have animal remnants in their couture. It's despicable, like having somebody's scalps on your sleeves. Obviously, that fits into the political issues of the play. Animals' rights are being taken away, but the people of Oz let it happen because the Wizard keeps them wealthy and entertained. Politics are at the heart of this play. I know that *Wicked* deals with it on a very simple level. But it was really important for all of us designers to hold on to it, instead of simply telling a funny story. I think it's one of the reasons the show moves people: They're recognizing a struggle between good and bad.

Glinda is the epitome of good, so I did research by asking little girls what goodness looks like. They said like a princess, like a bride. I collected and studied pictures of Queen Elizabeth II from her coronation, Lady Diana's wedding dress, and all of the dresses that are emblematic of perfect femininity. When you look at any of the English coronation images, it's hysterical, because it's all about impressing in a certain way. Even Queen Elizabeth, in the 1950s, wore a crown and a long robe and held her scepter, and I wanted to tap into that. Glinda is also connected to the sky, sun, and stars. That influenced her tiara and wand. The sparkles on her dress are all about that, too. She symbolizes lightness, air, bubbles. Kristin is someone you know loves costumes, because she comes from a beauty pageant background.

She can wear any kind of heel, and she knows makeup and hair. But she wanted to be transformed to be Glinda. We did a lot of fittings. I had to find just the right proportion in her Glinda dress, because she is tiny, tiny, tiny. She can get swallowed up in a second. It's like, one ruffle too many and you're over the top.

Elphaba is exactly the opposite. I see her as connected to things that are inside the earth. So the patterns and textures I wove into her dress include fossils, stalactites, or striations that you see when you crack a stone apart. I mixed different colors into her skirt, so everything is literally twisted. And there was no issue with Idina about whether a costume was or wasn't flattering. Idina is unbelievably gorgeous, but she's not at all obsessed with her looks. When I designed her clothes for Shiz, I gave her heavy boots, so right away she's connected to the earth, and then a cap that she pulls down low. Plus, she keeps her hands in her pockets. Idina completely embraced the idea of a young girl trying to hide herself. Now, by the time she gets to the Emerald City, she feels she belongs. I change her shoes so that she has a lighter pair. We take her glasses away, her hair comes down, and she's wearing a lighter color. And suddenly she feels accepted and even, you could say, fashionable. Glinda tells her at the end of Act I not to be afraid and she answers, "I'm not."

SUSAN HILFERTY FITS ACTRESS LAURA DYSARCZYK

OUTFITTING

WICKED

The CAPTIVATING COSTUMES *of*

SUSAN HILFERTY

In Susan Hilferty's bustling studio workshop on West 24th Street in New York, you will find shelves overflowing with books and drafting tables covered in papers. This is Hilferty's invaluable "image library," where the designer finds pictures that spark her imagination. Anything will serve: newspaper clippings, magazine photos, or illustrations in books. For the intensive researching and visualization needed to create the astonishing costumes of *Wicked*, Hilferty searched far and wide, from the contemporary fashion design of John Galliano to the Edwardian couture that she "twisted" to create many of *Wicked*'s unique Tony Award—winning costumes.

❧ ELPHABA ❧

From drab, sulky schoolgirl {BOTTOM LEFT} to formidable, sultry sorceress {TOP LEFT},
Elphaba makes an astonishing journey from girl to woman.

❖ GLINDA ❖

Glinda favors anything that's frilly and ultrafeminine. Her Shiz party look
{BOTTOM RIGHT} is pink and cute, but by the end of the play, she has blossomed into
a princess {TOP RIGHT}.

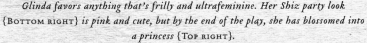

CHISTERY

When we first meet Chistery, he's just a Monkey in a butler's coat {TOP LEFT},
but Elphaba's spell transforms him into something much more exotic:
a Flying Monkey {BOTTOM LEFT}.

MADAME MORRIBLE

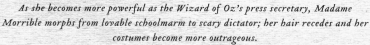

SHIZ UNIVERSITY

Student fashion at Shiz University looks diverse and highly individualist, but that's an illusion: all of the outfits are school uniforms, using the same Shiz blue-and-white striped pattern; the design is, however, eclectic and marked by dramatic asymmetry.

THE EMERALD CITY

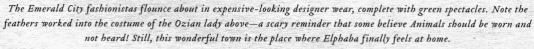

The Emerald City fashionistas flounce about in expensive-looking designer wear, complete with green spectacles. Note the feathers worked into the costume of the Ozian lady above—a scary reminder that some believe Animals should be worn and not heard! Still, this wonderful town is the place where Elphaba finally feels at home.

Part Four

FACE TIME

 **I**F YOU PASSED ANY OF THE ACTORS FROM *WICKED* ON THE STREET, CHANCES ARE YOU WOULDN'T RECOGNIZE THEM. OK, MAYBE KRISTIN CHENOWETH'S BLOND LOCKS AND 100-WATT SMILE OR IDINA MENZEL'S DARK EYES AND CHISELED CHEEKBONES WOULD CAUSE A FLUTTER OF RECOGNITION, but on the whole, the performers are masked under layers of makeup, not to mention wigs and prosthetic features (if they play Animals). Since the set and costumes of *Wicked* had to conjure up a fantastic world that seemed so unlike our own, the makeup also had to create a distinct look to distinguish each character. And of course, that

It didn't look flat or matte. Then, during one of Idina's lunch breaks, we sat down and I started applying it. It looked OK, but neither of us was really happy with it. Then I realized it would take a really long time to do every night. If anything happened and we had to do it quickly, there would be problems. And there was another major issue: makeup particles flying through the air.

ELPHABA IS NOT SUPPOSED TO BE UGLY, SHE'S SUPPOSED TO BE BEAUTIFUL. PEOPLE JUST HATE HER BECAUSE SHE'S GREEN.

—JOSEPH DULUDE II

was the makeup designer's greatest challenge: making Elphaba green, but not in a way that would make the actress uncomfortable or would fade as she sweated or interacted with the other characters. This is where cosmetic alchemist Joseph Dulude II enters, mixing his powders and creams to find the perfect formula.

JOSEPH DULUDE II (*Makeup Designer*): For Elphaba, I wanted a true green, an emerald green—not too yellow, not too blue. At first, I tried airbrushing, because it gives really nice coverage but it looks like skin.

That's not good for me, and it's also not good for Idina, because she has to sing. So, before we left for San Francisco tryouts, Idina and I went to the MAC Cosmetics store and got the Landscape Green Chromacake, which I had used before. I knew it would just look dark, but I diluted it a bit and then buffed and rubbed it out. Then we used purple shadows for contour, so it would be a nice contrast. And she really liked it, because she didn't feel like she was wearing a lot of makeup. It evolved a lot from there, but that was the basic idea. These days, I think my record for "greenifying" Elphaba is seven minutes.

Here's the process: I use these wide Japanese brushes that you can get in any art store, and I paint the green on. I do the face and the jawline first, and then I take a larger brush and buff it out. When you first put it on, it's wet and a little streaky, and sometimes it collects more in some places than it does in others. Then I do the neck area. And then I get in with the smaller brush and do the hairline and the ears and all of that. Then I use a water-proof powder and powder her all over and then brush the powder off. Then I start doing the regular makeup: eyeliner and purple and brown contours for the eyes and cheekbones. In Act I, Elphaba is supposed to look simple, like a young woman. So, there's some contouring and lining of the eyes, highlighting, filling in the eyebrows, and filling in the lips with a stone-colored pencil. And then she's brushed all over with Golden Olive pigment, but just on the face. That's basically her Act I look.

Then I start on her hands. And we only have to go a little bit up on her arms, because she wears a green bodysuit. Then I really powder those well. The powder helps, and then we spray a fixative on the hands. That really helps. If you see her up close, you can see that some of the green rubs off of the fingertips, because maybe she's holding on to the broom really tightly. It doesn't rub off on people's costumes.

I don't see Elphaba again until intermission. That's when we glam everything up. We arch and extend her eyebrows. We smudge the eyeliner, put some lashes on, increase the contour on her eyes, cheeks, and jawline and use this Green Derma color from Krylon, which is water-resistant as well. We put that on her lips and then powder it down. And then I just touch up her neck and her hands, then add powder and the spray fixative again. In Act II, she's more witchy, but in a glamorous way. Elphaba is not supposed to be ugly, she's supposed to be beautiful. People just hate her because she's green.

Madame Morrible was also fun to design. Carole Shelley, who originated the role on Broadway, is amazing. She and I worked a lot together and brought our own inspirations to the look. In Act I, she seems sweet and grandmotherly. She just wears crazy makeup. But then as the show continues, you realize that Morrible

Joe Dulude preps Idina Menzel before a show; the makeup artist's record for applying the Elphaba green look is seven minutes.

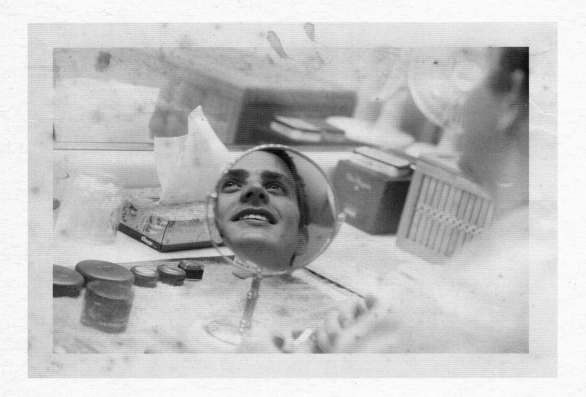

isn't really that sweet. She has had this plan from the beginning and just wants power and to use Elphaba. So the makeup translates, making her look rather mean, with dramatic makeup and a receded hairline with the harsh, pulled-back bun in the back. Susan Hilferty and I really went for a look that was inspired by Queen Elizabeth I, who was very regal and imposing, with tons of white makeup and blush.

Everyone in the show, chorus people included, wears makeup. For example, in the Act II Witch Hunters scene, Susan wanted them all to look kind of haggard and bruised, as if they hadn't gotten sleep. So we gave the actors a bunch of purple and blue makeup and just let them go to town. We gave them a guide of what they had to do, like dark circles under their eyes, or bruised cheeks, or things like that. And the lighting is so extreme in that scene. But we have this great scene where all these people come out, and they just look really frightening. And, you know, the Emerald City guards in the beginning look pretty normal. But then when they come out in Act II, after you find out that the Wizard is not the nice guy you thought he was, they all sort of have these dark circles under their eyes, and they look a little meaner.

Besides all that makeup, I also have to supervise a dozen or so foam-latex masks that were designed by Matthew Mungle. That includes Doctor Dillamond, the Flying Monkeys, and the other Animals in the show, like the Rat waiter and the Antelope midwife in the early scene when Elphaba is born. That means a little touching up here and there, because there's a lot of wear and tear on the masks from week to week.

People always ask if the actress playing Elphaba develops a skin rash or acne because of all that green makeup, and the answer is no. It's a water-based product; there's no oil in it. So it's gentle on the skin. You can go in the shower and use soap and it comes right off. I mean, some places, of course, you have to scrub a little bit more—like the hairline and inside the ears. But a lot of it is psychological, too. If you feel like you're wearing a lot of makeup, it can make you feel uncomfortable. "Oh, God, I have all this stuff on my face." You can forget about it and go on with the show.

Everyone in the show, chorus people included, wears makeup. Here, Joey McIntyre, who played "Fiyero" on Broadway, gets ready.

Tom Watson's
Wonderful Wigs

Carole Shelley wigs out (above), as she prepares her flamboyant Madame Morrible look. *Wicked* is a wig-heavy show. In each performance, 70 wigs are used, with actors making up to eight changes from beginning to end. And these aren't your cheap Halloween headpieces: Each is custom-built by designer Tom Watson and can cost anywhere from $1,200 to $2,400. All of the wigs are also "hand ventilated," meaning individual human hair strands are inserted manually, one at a time. Supervisor of the hair department Al Annotto admits that there is one synthetic wig in the show. "I dare you to guess which one it is," he says.

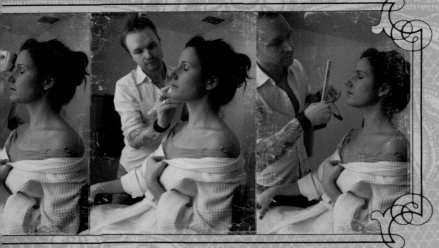

STEP ONE:

Joe Dulude works his magic with Stephanie J. Block on the *Wicked* national tour. In terms of skin preparation, Joe recommends that the actress not wash her face or moisturize before the "greenifying," since that could affect how the makeup goes on. First, he applies a color foundation. Then, using a wide Japanese brush (you can find them at any art store) he paints her using MAC Chromacake in Landscape Green. Joe applies it to the face and the jawline first, then takes a larger brush to smooth it out. Joe uses a smaller detailing brush to fill in the hairline and the ears. Then he applies a waterproof powder and starts on the regular makeup: eyeliner and purple and brown contours for the eyes and cheekbones. Finally, the actress's face is brushed with Golden Olive pigment to add some sparkle, and a spray fixative is applied to the hands to keep the makeup from rubbing off.

STEP TWO:

During intermission, Stephanie reports back to Joe for her Act II look, when she gets the "glam" treatment, so she looks older, sexier, and just plain witchier. He arches and extends her eyebrows. He smudges the eyeliner, puts lashes on, increases the contour on her cheeks and jawline, uses a Green Derma color from Krylon for her lips, and then powders her again. He touches up her neck and her hands, then powders them and sprays fixative all over again.

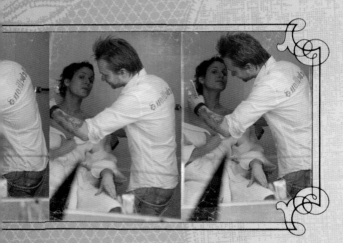

STEP THREE:

You might think that wearing that much makeup night after night would irritate the skin, but the MAC Chromacake is water-based, it contains no oils, so it's gentle on the skin. After each performance, the actress playing Elphaba can easily wash off the green. Joe recommends taking some Neutrogena into the shower. Watch out, though: some areas, such as the hairline and inside the ears, might take a little extra scrubbing!

making
ELPHABA
green

Tom Watson's
Wonderful Wigs

Carole Shelley wigs out (above), as she prepares her flamboyant Madame Morrible look. *Wicked* is a wig-heavy show. In each performance, 70 wigs are used, with actors making up to eight changes from beginning to end. And these aren't your cheap Halloween headpieces: Each is custom-built by designer Tom Watson and can cost anywhere from $1,200 to $2,400. All of the wigs are also "hand ventilated," meaning individual human hair strands are inserted manually, one at a time. Supervisor of the hair department Al Annotto admits that there is one synthetic wig in the show. "I dare you to guess which one it is," he says.

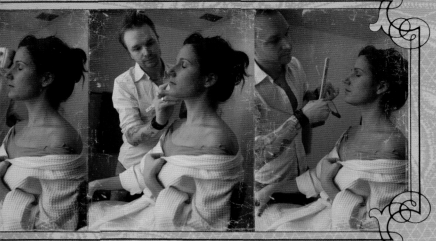

STEP ONE:

Joe Dulude works his magic with Stephanie J. Block on the *Wicked* national tour. In terms of skin preparation, Joe recommends that the actress not wash her face or moisturize before the "greenifying," since that could affect how the makeup goes on. First, he applies a color foundation. Then, using a wide Japanese brush (you can find them at any art store) he paints her using MAC Chromacake in Landscape Green. Joe applies it to the face and the jawline first, then takes a larger brush to smooth it out. Joe uses a smaller detailing brush to fill in the hairline and the ears. Then he applies a waterproof powder and starts on the regular makeup: eyeliner and purple and brown contours for the eyes and cheekbones. Finally, the actress's face is brushed with Golden Olive pigment to add some sparkle, and a spray fixative is applied to the hands to keep the makeup from rubbing off.

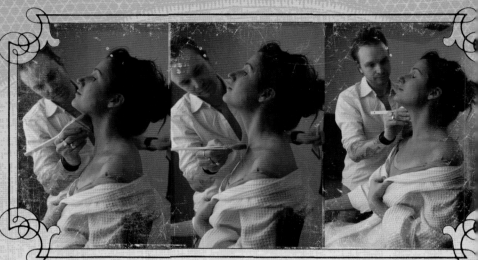

STEP TWO:

During intermission, Stephanie reports back to Joe for her Act II look, when she gets the "glam" treatment, so she looks older, sexier, and just plain witchier. He arches and extends her eyebrows. He smudges the eyeliner, puts lashes on, increases the contour on her cheeks and jawline, uses a Green Derma color from Krylon for her lips, and then powders her again. He touches up her neck and her hands, then powders them and sprays fixative all over again.

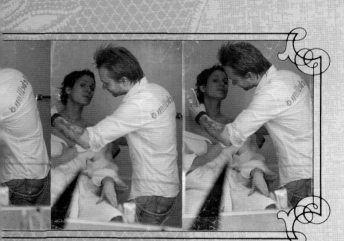

making ELPHABA green

STEP THREE:

You might think that wearing that much makeup night after night would irritate the skin, but the MAC Chromacake is water-based, it contains no oils, so it's gentle on the skin. After each performance, the actress playing Elphaba can easily wash off the green. Joe recommends taking some Neutrogena into the shower. Watch out, though: some areas, such as the hairline and inside the ears, might take a little extra scrubbing!

After ✑

Before ✑

Part Five

DANCE FEVER

ust as every note in Stephen Schwartz's score is there for a reason, and every line in Winnie Holzman's script serves a purpose, each actor's moves have been carefully worked out and choreographed. With a production as mammoth and finely designed as *WICKED*, in which the lights, set pieces, and special effects are controlled by computers, which in turn are run by a crew of stage managers and technicians, an actor wandering away from his or her mark onstage can create serious problems. In the wings, the areas to the left and right of the stage, actors and tech people have to keep out of one another's way, unless they want to get mowed down by a Glinda doing a lightning-fast costume change or a large and dangerous piece of set sliding into place. Wayne Cilento created the musical staging for *Wicked*. That means he was the crucial link between director Joe Mantello, who had to keep his eyes on the big picture, and Stephen Schwartz, whose music keeps the pulse of the show going. Need a dance here? Cilento stepped in. But he also helped to shape the particular quality of more mundane movement in the show.

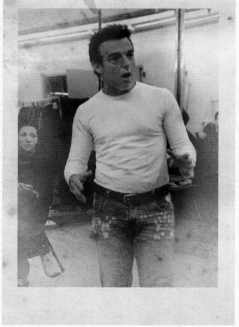

and the music was so interesting, but they weren't sure if the show needed choreography. But when I listened to it, I knew that Oz had to move and dance, to create an atmosphere and an environment. It wasn't just about doing production numbers, like with most Broadway shows—the cast just breaking into dance. The choreography needed to keep the story moving. So I would lay down the movement road map, and Joe would insert his thoughts and directing ideas about what story we were telling, and then I would physicalize it with the actors. I don't think people really understand what a choreographer does. It's not just dance steps. Joe and I worked out the transitions together, which turned into choreographic moments. The opening, "No One Mourns the Wicked," is just constant choreography. That kind of choreography is almost harder than just doing a dance number, since it's character-driven. "What Is This Feeling," which starts with Glinda and Elphaba and brings in all the students in sort of a backup-dancing chorus, is one of those numbers that's not about dancing, per se, but telling a story.

In general, the movements I created for the actors

WAYNE CILENTO (*Musical Staging*): If the collaboration is successful, you don't know where the direction starts and the choreography ends. The whole thing is a collaboration between Joe and me. When I went to see an early reading, I thought the show was so unique,

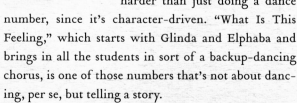

WAYNE CILENTO

THERE'S A WHOLE RANGE OF DANCE STYLES IN *WICKED* THAT A LAYPERSON WOULDN'T REALIZE. TO REALLY EXECUTE THE MUSICAL STAGING, YOU NEED AN EXTREMELY TALENTED ENSEMBLE.

—WAYNE CILENTO

were deliberately off center. For Elphaba it was fluid, a lot of hand and upper-body movement—magical, spell-casting movement. Glinda was perky, like a showgirl or a contestant in a beauty pageant. Fiyero was lanky and loose-limbed. His movement vocabulary was coming from a scarecrow, where it was very angular and without joints. Actors who had a modern-dance background played the Flying Monkeys. There's a whole range of dance styles in *Wicked* that a layperson wouldn't realize. To really execute the musical staging, you need an extremely talented ensemble. An ensemble

member can't get away with just dancing anymore: You have to be able to sing and act.

Basically, it's not a dance show, yet there's dancing nonstop. The battle was to make it dancey but not dancey. Make it move but camouflage it. So there was no time to sit there and just dance. Except, obviously, in scenes like "Dancing Through Life."

I wanted Elphaba's dance in the Ozdust Ballroom to be whimsical, and the swirling arm movements were there to suggest casting spells on someone. Idina and I worked together and made a dance out of it, which the

of the Wicked Witch of the West, but it's not a replica. A lot of it is logistical. We were always asking ourselves, "What do we need to tell the story in the scene?" When Glinda and Elphaba go to the Wizard's chamber we had to deliver certain spectacular effects, but for the classroom scene, maybe the students are simply sitting on two benches—you reduce it to what's absolutely necessary. I would always tell the designers, we're being called upon to create our own version of Oz. With the set design, I knew that we wanted to take a cue from Gregory's novel and also reference the film a bit. And come up with something that was completely original. So, obviously, *Wicked*'s look and sound is darker than the film, but the musical isn't the novel, so there had to be moments when we really delivered a Broadway show.

rest of the ensemble picks up, and it becomes the Elphaba Dance. It is also very psychologically revealing: She's closing herself off and opening up at the same time.

The Wizard and Elphaba waltz in "Wonderful" came from vaudeville. Once again, every time there's a different actor playing the Wizard, I have to mold it to them. Joel Grey is Joel Grey, so he has a particular way of moving. George Hearn [who also played the Wizard on Broadway] is really not a dancer, but he's a fantastic actor. So, I catered it to him. It's interesting to mold the dance to different actors who come into the roles.

JOE MANTELLO (*on how the design, sound, and dance came together*): The first piece of the puzzle was the set. Eugene came in with a large, white model, which served as the basis for what we have now, though it was completely rethought. His idea of exposing the mechanics of the world was there from the beginning. With Susan Hilferty, we looked at W. W. Denslow illustrations from the original Baum books and at John Galliano couture designs. That's where some of the ideas of the asymmetry came from. We had to take the iconic images that people knew and give them a twist. So Elphaba's Act II costume references what we know

{TOP} STEPHEN OREMUS, JOE MANTELLO, AND WAYNE CILENTO BREAK DOWN SOME MOVES
When he's not rehearsing a new cast, Cilento returns to the Broadway production of Wicked *to make sure the dance and movement is as fresh as ever. If he's not available to conduct a "clean up" rehearsal, his two dance captains are always on hand to watch shows and take notes. "We're always touching up the dance in the show," Cilento says. "And there are constant understudy rehearsals, introducing new cast members who are playing principal parts. It just never stops."*

{BOTTOM} *Robb Sapp and Dance Captain Mark Myars brush up on some moves during a* Wicked *rehearsal.*

A new craze is sweeping the dance floors, a hot new trend started by Elphaba at the Ozdust Ballroom. *Wicked* choreographer Wayne Cilento explains the dance in six easy steps. He found inspiration by the fact that Elphaba is a witch and tried to find a lyrical, internal way of moving.

STEP 1

With her feet planted firmly apart, Elphaba stands up straight. Her hands swirl around each other—she's casting a lyrical spell, so they're "soft hands."

STEP 2

Now she's fantasizing about things that could happen—at Shiz, in her life. The next movement is a rotation of the head.

STEP 3

The physical scope of her dance gets bigger, she lifts her hands from a low position to a high position and then circles them down to the floor, bringing focus to her feet.

STEPS 4 & 5

Step 5

Step 4

She extends her left leg. She leans toward the leg, sweeps her body around, and comes back to the front. Then (Step 5) we bring the movement into the lower part of her body, her arms are still casting spells, and she circles her hips.

(Step 6) She makes a turn and starts it all over again . . .

"I hear her soul is so unclean, pure water can melt her . . .
Please—somebody go and melt her!"

—ANGRY OZIANS {IN REFERENCE TO ELPHABA}

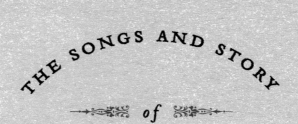

THE SONGS AND STORY

of

WICKED

PART ONE

CHAPTER I

OUR STORY BEGINS OUTSIDE THE WIZARD'S PALACE, IN THE EMER-
ALD CITY, CAPITAL OF THE LAND OF OZ, WHERE A THRILLIFYING
CELEBRATION IS TAKING PLACE.

ALL: Good news! / She's dead! / The Witch of the West is dead! / The wickedest witch there ever was / The enemy of all us here in Oz / Is dead! / Good news! / Good news!

SOMEONE IN THE CROWD: Look! It's Glinda!

Glinda, resplendent and beautiful in her gown and tiara, descends from the sky on a mechanical device that spews soap bubbles.

VARIOUS FANATICS: Is it really her? It is, it's her! Glinda! We love yeeew, Glindaaaaa!

GLINDA: It's good to see me, isn't it? No need to respond—that was rhetorical. Fellow Ozians—
Let us be glad / Let us be grateful / Let us rejoicify that Goodness could subdue / The wicked workings of you-know-who / Isn't it nice to know / That good will conquer evil? / The truth we all believe'll by and by / Outlive a lie / For you and—

SOMEONE IN THE CROWD: Glinda! Exactly how dead is she?

GLINDA: Because there has been so much rumor and speculation—innuendo, outuendo—let me set the record straight: According to the Time Dragon Clock, The Melting occurred at the thirteenth hour, the direct result of a bucket of water thrown by a female child. Yes, the Wicked Witch of the West is dead.

SOMEONE ELSE IN THE CROWD: No one mourns the wicked

ANOTHER PERSON: No one cries: "They won't return!"

ALL: No one lays a lily on their grave

MAN: The good man scorns the wicked!

WOMEN: Through their lives, our children learn:

ALL: What we miss / When we misbehave . . .

GLINDA: And goodness knows / The wicked's lives are lonely / Goodness knows / The wicked die alone / It just shows when you're wicked / You're left only / On your own . . .

ALL: Yes, goodness knows / The wicked's lives are lonely / Goodness knows / The wicked cry alone / Nothing grows for the wicked / They reap only / What they've sown . . .

GIRL IN THE CROWD: Glinda, why does Wickedness happen?

GLINDA: That's a good question. One that many people find confusifying: Are people born Wicked? Or do they have Wickedness thrust upon them? After all, she had a childhood. She had a father . . . who just happened to be the Governor of Munchkinland . . .

From out of the past appears a somber-looking man: the Witch's Father.

WITCH'S FATHER: I'm off to the Assembly, dear!

GLINDA: And she had a mother. As so many do . . .

A hauntingly beautiful woman rushes to the somber man's side: the Witch's Mother.

WITCH'S FATHER: Oh . . . how I hate to go and leave you lonely

"IT'S GOOD TO SEE ME, ISN'T IT?"

"LIKE A FROGGY, FERNY CABBAGE, THE BABY IS UNNATURALLY . . . GREEN!"

WITCH'S MOTHER: That's alright—it's only just one night

WITCH'S FATHER: But know that you're here in my heart / While I'm out of your sight . . .

The Father leaves, and instantly, the Mother wipes his kiss from her cheek. She opens a door . . .

GLINDA: And like every family—they had their secrets.

And her Lover, a mysterious man whose face remains in the shadow, appears.

LOVER: Have another drink, my dark-eyed beauty / I've got one more night left here in town / So have another drink of green elixir / And we'll have ourselves a little mixer / Have another little swallow, little lady, / And follow me down . . .

They kiss; sink to the floor. The Lover disappears. The Mother struggles back to her feet, now hugely pregnant—

GLINDA: But, from the moment she was born she was . . . well, different.

Suddenly the Witch's Mother clutches herself, in pain . . .

WITCH'S MOTHER: Agghhh!!

The Witch's Father rushes in, along with a Midwife, who happens to be an Antelope. They hold her—

MIDWIFE: It's coming . . .

WITCH'S FATHER: Now?

MIDWIFE: The baby's coming . . .

WITCH'S FATHER: And how!

MIDWIFE: I see a nose . . .

WITCH'S FATHER: I see a curl . . .

MIDWIFE AND WITCH'S FATHER: It's a healthy perfect lovely little . . .

MIDWIFE: Ohhhhh!

WITCH'S FATHER: Sweet Oz!

WITCH'S MOTHER: What is it? What's wrong?

MIDWIFE: How can it be?

WITCH'S FATHER: What does it mean?

MIDWIFE: It's atrocious!

WITCH'S FATHER: It's obscene!

MIDWIFE AND WITCH'S FATHER : Like a froggy, ferny cabbage / The baby is unnaturally—

ALL: Green!!

WITCH'S FATHER: Take it away. Take *it* away . . . !

GLINDA: So you see—it couldn't have been easy!

CROWD: No one mourns the wicked / Now at last, she's dead and gone / Now at last, there's joy throughout the land / And Goodness knows

GLINDA: Goodness knows . . .

CROWD: We know what goodness is

GLINDA: Her life was lonely . . .

CROWD: Goodness knows . . .

GLINDA: Goodness knows . . .

CROWD: The wicked die alone . . .

GLINDA: She died alone . . .

CROWD: Woe to those / Who spurn what goodness is / They are shown / No one mourns the wicked . . .

GLINDA: Good news!

CROWD: No one mourns the wicked!

GLINDA: Good news!

CROWD: No one mourns the / wicked! / wicked!

ALL: wicked!

"IT'S OBSCENE! . . . TAKE *IT* AWAY!"

GLINDA: Well, this has been fun. But as you can imagine, I have much to attend to, what with the Wizard's unexpected departure. And so, if there are no further questions—

Suddenly, someone in the crowd interrupts her.

PERSON IN THE CROWD: Glinda! Is it true—you were her friend?!

The crowd gasps in disbelief. Glinda freezes, completely thrown. And once again, the past comes alive. For Glinda suddenly sees—her friend Elphaba, just as she was on the day that Galinda (as she was known then) first laid eyes on her: young, hopeful, and . . . green.

CHAPTER II

I N A PARLOR AT SHIZ UNIVERSITY, *the incoming students gather. Galinda is the last to arrive, perched on an enormous stack of luggage.*

STUDENTS: O hallowed halls and vine-draped walls . . . The proudliest sight there is / When grey and sere our hair hath turned / We shall still revere the lessons learned / In our days at dear old Shiz / Our days at dear old . . .

GALINDA: Oh-oh-oh-oh-old . . .

STUDENTS & GALINDA: Dear old Shiz-zzzz . . .

Galinda and all the other students rudely gape at Elphaba. Finally she can't take it anymore—

ELPHABA: What? What are you all looking at? Oh—do I have something in my teeth? Alright, fine—we might as well get this over with: No, I'm not seasick; yes, I've always been green; no, I didn't eat grass as a child . . .

Elphaba's Father scolds her for making a scene and reminds her to take care of her sister Nessarose, who is in a wheelchair. Meanwhile, Galinda is thrilled to shreds to meet Madame Morrible, the school's headmistress and a renowned sorceress, with whom Galinda wishes to study sorcery. Madame Morrible announces the room assignments, and Galinda and Elphaba are quite distressed to learn that they will room together. Elphaba is particularly shaken, as she assumed she would room with her sister, the better to fulfill her promise to her Father. As Madame Morrible starts to wheel Nessarose away, Elphaba loses control and makes something magical occur. Nessarose is mortified, but when Elphaba tries to apologize . . .

MORRIBLE: What?! Never apologize for talent! Talent is a gift! And that is my special talent, encouraging talent! Have you ever considered a career in sorcery?

ELPHABA: Not really . . .

MORRIBLE: I shall tutor you privately—and take no other students!
Many years I have waited / For a gift like yours to appear / Why, I predict the Wizard could make you his / Magic Grand Vizier!

ELPHABA: The Wizard!?

MORRIBLE: My dear, my dear / I'll write at once to the Wizard— / Tell him of you in advance / With a talent like yours, dear / There is a defin-ish chance / If you work as you should— / You'll be making good . . .

The crowd disperses and Elphaba is left alone, dazed but thrilled.

ELPHABA: Did that really just happen? / Have I actually understood? / This weird quirk I've tried / To suppress or hide / Is a talent that could / Help me meet the Wizard / If I make good / So I'll make good . . . /

When I meet the Wizard / Once I prove my worth / And then I meet the Wizard / What I've waited for since— since birth! / And with all his Wizard wisdom / By my looks, he won't be blinded / Do you think the Wizard is dumb? / Or like Munchkins, so small-minded? / No! He'll say to me: / "I see who you truly are / A girl on whom I can rely!" / And that's how we'll begin / The Wizard and I . . . /

Once I'm with the Wizard / My whole life will change / 'Cuz once you're with the Wizard / No one thinks you're strange / No father is not proud of you / No sister acts ashamed / And all of Oz has to love you / When by the Wizard, you're acclaimed / And this gift—or this curse— / I have inside / Maybe at last, I'll know why / When we are hand in hand— / The Wizard and I! /

And one day, he'll say to me: "Elphaba, / A girl who is so superior / Shouldn't a girl who's so good inside / Have a matching exterior? / And since folks here to an absurd degree / Seem fixated on your verdigris / Would it be all right by you / If I de-greenify you?" / And though of course that's not important to me / "All right, why not?" I'll reply / Oh, what a pair we'll be / The Wizard and I . . . / Yes, what a pair we'll be / The Wizard and . . .

Unlimited! / My future is unlimited / And I've just had a vision / Almost like a prophecy / I know—it sounds truly crazy / And true, the vision's hazy / But I swear, someday there'll be / A celebration throughout Oz / That's all to do with me! / And I'll stand there with the Wizard / Feeling things I've never felt / And though I'd never show it / I'll be so happy, I could melt / And so it will be / For the rest of my life / And I'll want nothing else till I die / Held in such high esteem / When people see me, they will scream / For half of Oz's fav'rite team: / The Wizard / And I!

"MANY YEARS I HAVE WAITED FOR A GIFT LIKE YOURS TO APPEAR."

CHAPTER III

ALINDA AND ELPHABA ARE IN their dormitory room, both dutifully writing home.

GALINDA: Dearest darlingest Momsie and Popsical . . .

ELPHABA: My dear Father . . .

BOTH: There's been some confusion / Over rooming here at Shiz . . .

ELPHABA: But of course, I'll care for Nessa . . .

GALINDA: But of course, I'll rise above it . . .

BOTH: For I know that's how you'd want me to respond / Yes, there's been some confusion / For you see, my roommate is . . .

GALINDA: Unusually and exceedingly peculiar and altogether quite impossible to describe . . .

ELPHABA: Blonde.

GALINDA: What is this feeling / So sudden and new?

ELPHABA: I felt the moment / I laid eyes on you

GALINDA: My pulse is rushing . . .

ELPHABA: My head is reeling . . .

GALINDA: My face is flushing . . .

BOTH: What is this feeling? / Fervid as a flame / Does it have a name? / Yes!: / Loathing / Unadulterated loathing . . .

GALINDA: For your face . . .

ELPHABA: Your voice . . .

GALINDA: Your clothing . . .

BOTH: Let's just say—I loathe it all! / Ev'ry little trait, however small / Makes my very flesh begin to crawl / With simple utter loathing / There's a strange exhila-ration / In such total detestation / It's so pure! So strong! / Though I do admit it came on fast / Still I do believe that it can last / And I will be loathing / Loathing you / My whole life long!

STUDENTS:
Dear Galinda, you are just too good! / How do you stand it? I don't think I could! / She's a terror! She's a tartar! / We don't mean to show a bias / But Galinda you're a martyr!

GALINDA: Well . . . These things are sent to try us!

STUDENTS: Poor Galinda, forced to reside / With someone so disgusticified / We just want to tell you: / We're all on your side! / We share your . . .

GALINDA AND ELPHABA:	STUDENTS:
What is this feeling	Loathing
So sudden and new?	Unadulterated loathing
I felt the moment	For her face, her voice
I laid eyes on you	Her clothing
My pulse is rushing	Let's just say:
My head is reeling	We loathe it all!
Oh, what is this feeling?	Ev'ry little trait
	however small
Does it have a name?	Makes our very flesh
Yes . . .	Begin to crawl . . .
Ahhh . . .	Ahhh . . .

ALL: Loathing!

GALINDA AND ELPHABA:	STUDENTS:
There's a strange exhilaration	Loathing
In such total detestation	Loathing
So pure, so strong!	

STUDENTS: So strong!

GALINDA AND ELPHABA: Though I do admit it came on fast / Still I do believe that it can last

GALINDA AND ELPHABA:	STUDENTS:
And I will be loathing	Loathing
For forever loathing	Loathing
Truly, deeply loathing you	Loathing you
For my whole life long!	Loathing, unadulter-ated loathing

CHAPTER IV

N A LECTURE HALL, THE STUDENTS take their seats for Doctor Dillamond's class. Doctor Dillamond is a Goat. Today he is lecturing about Oz's political and social history, but as he turns his chalkboard around to pose a question, he sees that, across the board, someone has painted: "Animals should be seen and not heard." Dillamond, shocked, dismisses the class. Only Elphaba lingers, and offers her sandwich and her sympathy.

ELPHABA: You shouldn't let ignorant statements like that bother you. I mean, I always do, but you shouldn't.

DILLAMOND: Oh, Miss Elphaba— if only it were just a matter of words on a chalkboard! But the things one hears these days. Dreadful things . . .
I've heard of an Ox / A Professor from Quox / No longer permitted to teach / Who has lost all powers of speech . . .

ELPHABA: What?

DILLAMOND: And an Owl in Munchkin Rock / A vicar with a thriving flock / Forbidden to preach / Now he only can screech / Only rumors—but still— / Enough to give pause / To anyone with paws / Something bad is happening in Oz . . .

ELPHABA: Something bad? Happening in Oz . . . ?

DILLAMOND: Under the surface / Behind the scenes / Something baaaaaad . . .

They're both startled by an unfamiliar sound. It's coming from Doctor Dillamond himself—a kind of bleating. Dillamond hastily covers his mouth, clears his throat.

DILLAMOND: Bad.

ELPHABA: If something bad is happening to the Animals, someone's got to tell the Wizard! He'll make it right! That's why we *have* a Wizard—
So nothing bad . . .

DILLAMOND: I hope you're right—

BOTH: Nothing all that bad . . .

DILLAMOND: Nothing truly baaaaaaaad . . . / Sorry— bad . . .

Unsettled, Doctor Dillamond leaves the classroom. Elphaba watches him go . . .

ELPHABA: It couldn't happen here / In Oz . . . .

CHAPTER V

N THE COURTYARD, A NEW student arrives. Galinda realizes that this is Fiyero, the Winkie Prince with a reputation for "scandalaciousness." She is immediately drawn to him—in spite of a lovestruck Munchkin's best efforts to hold her interest. Fiyero asks Galinda and Boq (the Munchkin) what they do for fun, and before they can answer . . .

FIYERO: The trouble with schools is / They always try to teach the wrong lesson / Believe me, I've been kicked out / Of enough of them to know / They want you to become less callow / Less shallow / But I say: why invite stress in? / Stop studying strife / And learn to live "the unexamined life" . . .

Dancing through life / Skimming the surface / Gliding where turf is smooth / Life's more painless / For the brainless / Why think too hard? / When it's so soothing / Dancing through life / No need to tough it / When you can slough it off as I do / Nothing matters / But knowing nothing matters / It's just life / So keep dancing through . . .

Dancing through life / Swaying and sweeping / And always keeping cool / Life is fraught less / When you're thoughtless / Those who don't try / Never look foolish / Dancing through life . . . / Mindless and careless / Make sure you're where less / Trouble is rife / Woes are fleeting / Blows are glancing . . . / When you're dancing . . . / Through life . . .

So—what's the most swankified place in town?

GALINDA: That would be the Ozdust Ballroom.

FIYERO: Sounds perfect!
Let's go down to the Ozdust Ballroom / We'll meet there later tonight / We can dance till it's light / Find the prettiest girl . . . / Give 'er a whirl / Right on down to the Ozdust Ballroom / Come on—follow me / You'll be happy to be there . . .

ALL: Dancing through life / Down at the Ozdust . . .

FIYERO: If only because dust / Is what we come to . . .

ALL: Nothing matters / But knowing nothing matters / It's just life . . .

FIYERO: So keep dancing through . . . .

BOQ: Miss Galinda—I hope you'll save at least one dance for me. I'll be right there. Right by your side. Waiting. All night.

GALINDA: Oh—that's so kind—Bick.

BOQ: Boq.

GALINDA: But you know what would be even kinder? See that tragic'ly beautiful girl / The one in the chair / It seems so unfair / We should go on a spree / And not she / Gee— / I know someone would be my hero / If that someone were / To go invite her . . .

BOQ: Well, maybe—I could invite her!

GALINDA: Oh, Bick, really? You would do that for me!?

BOQ: I would do anything for you, Miss Galinda. Excuse me, Miss Nessarose? There's something I'd like to ask you . . .

Boq wheels Nessarose away. Fiyero approaches Galinda with admiration.

FIYERO: You're good.

GALINDA: I don't know what you mean! But I do happen to be free tonight, so...

FIYERO: . . . So I'll be picking you up around eight?

GALINDA: After all—
Now that we've met one another . . .

FIYERO AND GALINDA: It's clear—we deserve each other

GALINDA: You're perfect . . .

FIYERO: *You're* perfect . . .

BOTH: So we're perfect together / Born to be forever . . . / Dancing through life . . .

CHAPTER VI

ELPHABA, OBSERVING THE OTHER *students in this celebratory frenzy, expresses her disdain for Fiyero to Nessarose. Nessa confesses that she too is going to the dance, and it's all thanks to Elphaba's nemesis, Galinda.*

NESSAROSE: Fin'lly, for this one night / I'm about to have a fun night / With this Munchkin boy / Galinda found for me / And I only wish there were / Something I could do for her / To repay her / Elphaba, see? / We deserve each other / And Galinda helped it come true / We deserve each other / Me and Boq . . .

Please, Elphaba—try to understand . . .

ELPHABA: I do . . .

In the room she shares with Elphaba, Galinda prepares for the dance. Two mean girls, Pfannee and ShenShen, find a pointy black hat amongst Galinda's things, and they dare Galinda to give it to Elphaba to wear to the party. Elphaba comes to thank Galinda for her kindness to Nessarose, but before she can, Galinda proffers the hat.

GALINDA: It's really, uh, sharp, don't you think? / You know—black is this year's pink / You deserve each other / This hat and you / You're both so smart / You deserve each other / So here, out of the goodness of my heart . . .

Later, in the Ozdust Ballroom, Fiyero and Galinda dance as Boq and Nessarose look on.

BOQ: Listen—Nessa—

NESSAROSE: Yes?

BOQ: Uh—Nessa / I've got something to confess, a / Reason why, well—why I asked you here tonight / Now I know it isn't fair . . .

NESSAROSE: Oh, Boq. I know why.

BOQ: You do?

NESSAROSE: It's because I'm in this chair / And you felt sorry for me— / Well? Isn't that right?

BOQ: No! No! It's because . . . because . . .

"OUT OF THE GOODNESS OF MY HEART . . ."

"IT'S REALLY, UH, SHARP, DON'T YOU THINK?...YOU DESERVE EACH OTHER, THIS HAT AND YOU."

But he can't bring himself to tell her the truth.
Because you are so beautiful

NESSAROSE: Oh, Boq, I think you're wonderful! / And we deserve each other / Don't you see, this is our chance? / We deserve each other / Don't we, Boq?

BOQ: You know what? Let's dance!

NESSAROSE: What?

BOQ: Let's dance!

Boq begins to whirl a smitten Nessarose onto the dance floor when Elphaba walks in, wearing a pointy black hat. In a split second Elphaba realizes that Galinda has tricked her. The

other students laugh and point. Determined to ignore them, Elphaba closes her eyes and, all by herself, starts to dance.

Suddenly, Madame Morrible struts into the Ozdust and informs Galinda that she will at last be allowed to join the sorcery seminar. Galinda is overjoyed, but when she realizes that it's all due to Elphaba—who threatened to quit the seminar if she wasn't included—Galinda feels terrible for what she's done.

In a show of solidarity, she joins Elphaba on the dance floor.

ALL: Dancing through life / Down at the Ozdust / If only because dust / Is what we come to / And the strange thing: / Your life could end up changing / While you're dancing / Through!

CHAPTER VII

ACK IN THEIR DORMITORY ROOM, Elphaba and Galinda have been up all night, sharing their deepest secrets.

GALINDA: Look—it's tomorrow! And Elphie—is it all right if I call you Elphie?

ELPHABA: Well, it's a little perky.

GALINDA: And you can call me . . . Galinda. You see Elphie, now that we're friends, I've decided to make you my new project.

ELPHABA: You really don't have to do that.

GALINDA: I know. That's what makes me so nice!
Whenever I see someone / Less fortunate than I / And let's face it—who isn't / Less fortunate than I? / My tender heart / Tends to start to bleed / And when someone needs a makeover / I simply have to take over / I know *I* know exactly what they need / And even in your case / Tho' it's the toughest case I've yet to face / Don't worry—I'm determined to succeed / Follow my lead / And yes, indeed / You will be . . .

Popular! / You're gonna be popular! / I'll teach you the proper ploys / When you talk to boys / Little ways to flirt and flounce / I'll show you what shoes to wear / How to fix your hair / Everything that really counts to be popular! / I'll help you be popular! / You'll hang with the right cohorts / You'll be good at sports / Know the slang you've got to know / So let's start / 'Cause you've got an awf'lly long way to go . . .

Don't be offended by my frank analysis / Think of it as personality dialysis / Now that I've chosen to become a pal, a sis— / Ter and adviser / There's nobody wiser / Not when it comes to popular— / I know about popular / And with an assist from me / To be who you'll be / Instead of dreary who-you-were . . . are . . . / There's nothing that can stop you / From becoming popu- / Ler . . . lar . . . / La la la la / We're gonna make / You popular . . .

When I see depressing creatures / With unprepossessing features / I remind them on their own behalf / To think of / Celebrated heads of state or / 'Specially great communicators / Did they have brains or knowledge? / Don't make me laugh!

They were popular! Please— / It's all about popular! / It's not about aptitude / It's the way you're viewed / So it's very shrewd to be / Very very popular / Like me!

ELPHABA: This is never going to work . . .

GALINDA: Elphie! You mustn't think that way anymore! Your whole life is going to change! And all because of me! First: hair. See? This is how you toss your hair: Toss. Toss.

She demonstrates and Elphaba tries.

GALINDA: Well—you'll practice! And now—
She picks up her new magic wand—it's quite small, a training wand.
I shall transform your simple "frock" into a magnificent ball gown. Ball gown.

"YOU'LL BE POPULAR. JUST NOT QUITE AS POPULAR AS ME!"

She tries and fails, then examines the wand, puzzled. Is this thing on?

ELPHABA: You want me to try?

GALINDA: Oh, just wear the frock it's pretty! Oh—and this!

Galinda takes a flower from her own hair, pins it into Elphaba's.

GALINDA: Pink goes good with green. Why, Miss Elphaba—look at you. You're beautiful.

She guides her friend to a mirror. Elphaba stares at herself: For a moment it seems possible. And then—she forces herself to turn away.

ELPHABA: I—I have to go—

GALINDA: You're welcome!
And tho' you protest / Your disinterest / I know clandestinely / You're gonna grin and bear it / Your new-found popularity— / La la la la / You'll be popular / Just not quite as popular / As me!

CHAPTER VIII

OCTOR DILLAMOND'S LECTURE IS interrupted by Madame Morrible and several Ozian officials. She explains regretfully that Animals are no longer permitted to teach and that she therefore has no choice but to remove Doctor Dillamond at once. *Elphaba is stunned by this dreadful news. One official takes over the class, lecturing on a new scientific innovation: the cage. He reveals this device to the students. There is a small Lion Cub trapped inside. Elphaba becomes so distraught that she involuntarily casts a spell over the entire class—except for Fiyero. The two grab the cage and head out to the forest, where they set the Lion Cub free.*

Elphaba realizes that she could love Fiyero, yet she feels more alone than ever..

ELPHABA: Hands touch, eyes meet / Sudden silence, sudden heat / Hearts leap in a giddy whirl / He could be that boy / But I'm not that girl

Don't dream too far / Don't lose sight of who you are / Don't remember that rush of joy / He could be that boy / I'm not that girl

Ev'ry so often we long to steal / To the land of what-might-have-been / But that doesn't soften the ache we feel / When reality sets back in

Blithe smile, lithe limb / She who's winsome, she wins him / Gold hair with a gentle curl / That's the girl he chose / And heaven knows / I'm not that girl . . .

Don't wish, don't start / Wishing only wounds the heart / I wasn't born for the rose and pearl / There's a girl I know / He loves her so / I'm not that girl . . .

Madame Morrible comes upon Elphaba, taking shelter from the rain, and approaches her excitedly.

MORRIBLE: Oh, I have thrillifying news! I've finally heard back from the Wizard, and my dear—he wishes to meet you!

She makes a sudden dramatic gesture, and the rain instantly stops.

MORRIBLE: Oh, didn't I ever mention? Weather is my specialty. Oz speed, my dear.
Now you're off to meet the Wizard / Make me proud!

ELPHABA: I will—I'll try . . .
And there we'll finally be: / The Wizard and I . . .

 *ALINDA HAS ACCOMPANIED ELPHABA to the train station to bid her good-bye. All at once, Galinda breaks into tears, confiding to her friend that no matter what she does, Fiyero remains distant and moodified. She's even changed her name to Glinda—in a show of solidarity with the departed Doctor Dillamond—in the hopes that this would please Fiyero, but to no avail.*

In an effort to cheer her up, Elphaba invites Glinda to come with her. Glinda dries her eyes . . .

GLINDA: I've always wanted to see the Emerald City.

TOURISTS: One short day / In the Emerald City / One short day / In the Emerald City . . .

CHAPTER X

HE EMERALD CITY.

TOURISTS: One short day / In the Emerald City / One short day / Full of so much to do / Ev'ry way / That you look in this city / There's something exquisite / You'll want to visit / Before the day's through!

ELPHABA: There are buildings tall as quoxwood trees

GLINDA: Dress salons

ELPHABA: And libraries

GLINDA: Palaces!

ELPHABA: Museums!

BOTH: A hundred strong . . . / There are wonders like I've never seen

GLINDA: It's all grand

ELPHABA: And it's all green

BOTH: I think we've found the place where we belong! / I wanna be / In this hoi polloi

ELPHABA: So I'll be back for good someday

GLINDA: To make my life and make my way . . .

BOTH: But for today, we'll wander and enjoy . . .

ALL: One short day / In the Emerald City / One short day / To have a lifetime of fun / One short day . . .

ELPHABA AND GLINDA: And we're warning the city: / Now that we're in here / You'll know we've been here

ALL: Before we are done!

They are in front of a Broadway-style marquee that reads Wiz-o-mania. *Tourists pour into the theatre. Glinda takes in the scene, enthralled.*

GLINDA: The night-life! The hustle and bustle! It's all so . . . Ozmopolitan! Elphie, come on—we'll be late for *Wizomania!*

ELPHABA: I want to remember this moment. Always. Nobody's staring. Nobody's pointing. For the first time, I'm somewhere . . . where I belong.

GLINDA: You look positively—emerald!

They take each other's hands and run into the theatre.

WIZOMANIA CHORUS: Who's the mage / Whose major itinerary / Is making all Oz merrier? / Who's the sage / Who sagely sailed in to save / Our posteriors? / Whose enthuse for hot air ballooning / Has all of Oz honeymooning? / Woo-oo-oo . . . / Wiz-n't he wonderful? / (Our wonderful Wizard!)

"THE WIZARD WILL SEE YOU NOW!"

AUDIENCE:
One short day
In the Emerald
City
One short day
To have a lifetime of fun

ALL: What a way / To be seeing the city . . .

ELPHABA AND GLINDA: Where so many roam to /
We'll call it home too / And then, just like now / We
can say: / We're just two friends . . .

WIZOMANIA CHORUS:
Who's the mage
Whose major itinerary
Is making all Oz merrier
Who's the sage who
Sagely sailed in to save
Our posteriors . . .

ELPHABA: Two good friends . . .

GLINDA: Two *best* friends . . .

ALL: Sharing one wonderful /
One short . . .

GUARD: The Wizard will
see you now!

ALL: Day!

CHAPTER XI

*NSIDE THE WIZARD'S PRIVATE
chamber, Elphaba and Glinda come
face to face with the Wizard of Oz.*

ELPHABA: I'm so happy to meet
you.

WIZARD: Well, that's good—cuz that's what I love best
— making people happy.
I am a sentimental man / Who always longed to be a
father / That's why I do the best I can / To treat each
Citizen of Oz as son— / Or daughter . . . / So Elphaba,
I'd like to raise you high / 'Cuz I think ev'ryone
deserves / The chance to fly / And helping you with
your ascent al- / Lows me to feel so parental / For I
am a sentimental man . . .

*To the girls' amazement, Madame Morrible appears.
Surprisingly, she has become the Wizard's new press secretary. She holds an ancient looking book out to Elphaba.*

GLINDA: I don't believe it. Is that . . .
The Grimmerie!?

MORRIBLE: Yes. The Ancient Book of
Thaumaturgy and Enchantments.

ELPHABA: What funny writing.

MORRIBLE: It's a lost language—the lost
language of spells.

WIZARD: A kind of recipe book, for change.

*But when Elphaba realizes the Wizard has tricked her
into casting a spell on his caged pet Monkeys so that he can
use them as spies, she grabs The Grimmerie and runs from
the room. Glinda goes after her.*

"TELL THEM HOW I AM DEFYING GRAVITY. I'M FLYING HIGH . . ."

CHAPTER XII

HE GIRLS HAVE FLED TO THE uppermost turret of the Wizard's Palace and blockaded the door shut with an old broom.

GLINDA: Why couldn't you have stayed calm, for once! Instead of flying off the handle!
I hope you're happy / I hope you're happy now / I hope you're happy how you / Hurt your cause forever / I hope you think you're clever

ELPHABA: I hope *you're* happy / I hope you're happy too / I hope you're proud how you / Would grovel in submission / To feed your own ambition

BOTH: So though I can't imagine how / I hope you're happy right now . . .

GLINDA: Elphie, listen to me. Just say you're sorry. Before it's too late . . .
You can still be with the Wizard / What you've worked and waited for / You can have all you ever wanted . . .

ELPHABA: I know—
But I don't want it— / No—I *can't* want it / Anymore . . .

Something has changed within me / Something is not the same / I'm through with playing by the rules / Of someone else's game / Too late for second guessing / Too late to go back to sleep / It's time to trust my instincts / Close my eyes and leap

It's time to try / Defying gravity / I think I'll try / Defying gravity / And you can't pull me down . . .

GLINDA: Can't I make you understand, you're / Having delusions of grandeur . . . ?

ELPHABA: I'm through accepting limits / 'Cause someone says they're so / Some things I cannot change / But till I try, I'll never know / Too long I've been afraid of / Losing love I guess I've lost / Well, if that's love / It comes at much too high a cost / I'd sooner buy / Defying gravity / Kiss me goodbye / I'm defying gravity / And you can't pull me down . . .

GUARDS' VOICES: Open this door! In the name of His Supreme Ozness!

ELPHABA: Come with me. Think of what we could do . . . together.
Unlimited / Together we're unlimited / Together we'll be the greatest team / There's ever been / Glinda— / Dreams the way we planned 'em . . .

GLINDA: If we work in tandem . . .

BOTH: There's no fight we cannot win / Just you and I / Defying gravity / With you and I / Defying gravity

ELPHABA: They'll never bring us down . . .

Well? Are you coming?

The answer is no, but Glinda can't bring herself to say it. Instead, she gets an old black blanket from a shelf and wraps it around Elphaba's shoulders.

GLINDA: Elphie, you're trembling. Here . . . put this around you.
I hope you're happy / Now that you're choosing this . . .

ELPHABA: You too— / I hope it brings you bliss

BOTH: I really hope you get it / And you don't live to regret it / I hope you're happy in the end / I hope you're happy, my friend . . .

The palace guards burst in, their muskets drawn, as Elphaba rides her enchanted broom skyward.

ELPHABA: It's not her you want—It's me! It's meee!
So if you care to find me / Look to the western sky / As someone told me lately: / "Ev'ryone deserves the chance to fly" / And if I'm flying solo / At least I'm flying free / To those who'd ground me / Take a message back from me: / Tell them how I / Am defying gravity / I'm flying high / Defying gravity / And soon I'll match them in renown / And nobody in all of Oz / No Wizard that there is or was / Is ever gonna bring me down!

GLINDA: I hope you're happy!

CITIZENS OF OZ: Look at her, she's wicked! / Get her!

ELPHABA: . . . bring me down!

CITIZENS OF OZ: No one mourns the wicked / So we've got to bring her . . .

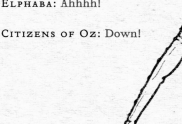

ELPHABA: Ahhhh!

CITIZENS OF OZ: Down!

"AND NOBODY IN ALL OF OZ—NO WIZARD THAT THERE IS OR WAS—
IS EVER GONNA BRING ME DOWN!"

PART TWO

TIME HAS PASSED, AND THE LAND OF OZ IS FILLED WITH FEAR.

CITIZENS OF OZ: Ev'ry day, more wicked! / Ev'ry day, the terror grows! / All of Oz is ever on alert! / That's the way with wicked— / Spreading fear / Where e'er she goes / Seeking out new victims she can hurt! / Like some terrible green blizzard / Throughout the land she flies . . . / Defaming our poor Wizard / With her calumnies and lies! / She lies! / Save us from the wicked! / Shield us so we won't be hexed! / Give us warning: where will she strike next? / Where will she strike next? / Where will she strike— / Next!?

CHAPTER XIII

UTSIDE THE WIZARD'S PALACE, Madame Morrible and Fiyero look on as a well-turned-out Glinda addresses an adoring crowd.

GLINDA: Fellow Ozians—as terrifying as terror is, let us put aside our panic for this one day and celebrate.
Oh what a celebration / We'll have today

CROWD: Thank goodness!

GLINDA: Let's have a celebration / The Glinda way . . .

CROWD: Thank goodness!

MORRIBLE:
Fin'lly a day that's / Totally Wicked-Witch-free!

CROWD: We couldn't be happier / Thank goodness!

Madame Morrible turns to Glinda and Fiyero, who's been named the new Captain of the Guard. She congratulates them on their engagement.

CROWD: Congratulotions!

FIYERO: This is an engagement party?

GLINDA: Surprised?

FIYERO: Yes!

GLINDA: Oh, good! We hoped you'd be—the Wizard and I! We couldn't be happier / Right, dear? / Couldn't be happier / Right here, look what we've got: / A fairy-tale plot / Our very own happy ending / Where we couldn't be happier / True, dear? / Couldn't be happier / And we're happy to share / Our ending vicariously / With all of you / He couldn't look handsomer / I couldn't feel humbler / We couldn't be happier / Because happy is what happens / When all your dreams come true!

MORRIBLE: And Glinda dear, we are happy for you! As Press Secretary, I've striven to ensure that all of Oz knows the story of your braverism! How vividly I remember . . .
The day you were first summoned / To an audience with Oz / And although he would not tell you why initially / When you bowed before his throne / He decreed you'd hence be known / As Glinda the Good—officially!

FIYERO: That's not how you described it to me!

GLINDA: Well, no, not exactly, but—

MORRIBLE: Then with a jealous squeal / The Wicked Witch burst from concealment / Where she had been lurking—surreptitially!

SOMEONE IN THE CROWD: I hear she has an extra eye / That always remains awake!

ANOTHER PERSON: I hear that she can shed her skin / As easily as a snake!

A THIRD PERSON: I hear some rebel animals / Are giving her food and shelter!

A FOURTH PERSON: I hear her soul is so unclean / Pure water can melt her!

FIYERO: What!?

CROWD: Melt her!? / Please—somebody go and melt her!

FIYERO: Do you hear that? Water will melt her!?

GLINDA: Fiyero—!

But Fiyero is disgusted and walks out on the celebration. Glinda tries to cover for her public.

GLINDA: Oh—yes, thanks plenty, dearest! He's gone to fetch me a refreshment. He's so thoughtful that way! That's why I couldn't be happier / No, I couldn't be happier / Though it is, I admit / The tiniest bit / Unlike I anticipated / But I couldn't be happier / Simply couldn't be happier / Well—not "simply"... / 'Cause getting your dreams / It's strange, but it seems / A little—well—complicated / There's a kind of a sort of . . . cost / There's a couple of things get . . . lost / There are bridges you cross / You didn't know you'd crossed / Until you've crossed . . .

And if that joy, that thrill / Doesn't thrill like you think it will / Still— / With this perfect finale / The cheers and the ballyhoo / Who / Wouldn't be happier? / So I couldn't be happier / Because happy is what happens / When all your dreams come true / Well, isn't it? / Happy is what happens . . . / When your dreams come true . . .

CROWD: We love you, Glinda, if we may be so frank . . .

GLINDA: Thank goodness!

CROWD: For all this joy, we know who we've got to thank: / Thank goodness!

MEN: That means, the Wizard . . .

WOMEN: Glinda . . .

GLINDA: And fiancé!

CROWD: They couldn't be goodlier / She couldn't be lovelier / We couldn't be luckier . . .

GLINDA: I couldn't be happier . . .

CROWD: Thank goodness . . .

GLINDA AND CROWD: Today! / Thank goodness for today!

"THANK GOODNESS!"

CHAPTER XIV

N THE GOVERNOR'S MANSION IN *Munchkinland, a uniformed Boq brings Nessarose of cup a tea. He has become her servant. Nessarose smiles up at him . . . ever hopeful. But Boq is formal and cold in response and hurries off, leaving Nessa alone and frustrated. All at once, Elphaba appears. She has been on the run for some time—a fugitive from justice. She has at last returned home, in hopes that her father might intercede on her behalf. So it comes as a shock when her sister informs her that her father is dead.*

Realizing that Nessarose has succeeded their father as Governor, Elphaba beseeches her sister for help, only to have Nessa turn on her.

NESSAROSE: All of my life, I depended on you / How do you think that feels? / All of my life, I've depended on you / And this hideous chair with wheels / Scrounging for scraps of pity to pick up / And longing to kick up / My heels . . .

ELPHABA: Wait—

She swiftly pulls The Grimmerie from her satchel and finds a spell.

NESSAROSE: What are you doing—what does that mean? Oh! Oh—my shoes!

And Nessarose's shoes begin to glow like fiery jewels. All at once, she miraculously stands up from her wheelchair.

ELPHABA: Oh, Nessa, at last / I've done what long ago I should / And finally from these powers, something good / Finally, something good!

Nessa calls out to Boq, and when he sees what's happened, he seizes his chance.

BOQ: Uh Nessa / Surely now I'll matter less to you / And you won't mind my leaving here tonight

NESSAROSE: Leaving?

BOQ: Yes — that ball that's being staged / Announcing Glinda is engaged . . .

NESSAROSE: Glinda.

BOQ: Yes, Nessa—that's right— / And I've got to go appeal to her / Express the way I feel to her— Oh, Nessa—I lost my heart to Glinda the moment I first saw her, you know that.

NESSAROSE: Lost your heart? Well—we'll see about that!

ELPHABA: Nessa—let him go—

NESSAROSE: Did you think I'd let you leave me here flat!?

BOQ: Don't come any closer!

NESSAROSE: You're going to lose your heart to me, I tell you / If I have to—I have to— / Magic spell you!

Nessarose grabs the book of spells.

NESSAROSE: Ah toom . . . Tah-take . . . ?

ELPHABA: Nessa, stop! It's dangerous!

NESSAROSE: Ah toom core tum!

BOQ: What, what's she doing? Oh! My heart—it feels like it's shrinking!

Nessa's spell takes hold of Boq and he collapses. Realizing what she's done, it's now Nessarose who begs for Elphaba's help.

NESSAROSE: Save him—please, just save him / My poor Boq, my sweet, my brave him / Don't leave me / Till my sorry life has ceased . . . / Alone and loveless here / With just the girl in the mirror / Just her and me— / The Wicked Witch of the East! / We deserve each other . . .

So Elphaba casts a spell of her own—to save his life, she turns him into a creature who can live without a heart.

And then she says goodbye to her sister for one last time.

"OH-MY SHOES!"

CHAPTER XV

NSIDE THE WIZARD'S CHAMBERS, Elphaba searches for the lever to the Monkey cage. Suddenly—the Wizard appears, asking her to give him another chance.

WIZARD: I never asked for this / Or planned it in advance / I was merely blown here / By the winds of chance / I never saw myself / As a Solomon or Socrates / I knew who I was: / One of your dime-a-dozen / Mediocrities / Then suddenly I'm here / Respected—worshipped even / Just because the folks in Oz / Needed someone to believe in / Does it surprise you / I got hooked, and all too soon? / What can I say? / I got carried away / And not just by balloon . . .

Wonderful / They called me "wonderful" / So I said "Wonderful—if you insist / I will be wonderful—" / And they said "Wonderful" / Believe me, it's hard to resist / 'Cause it feels wonderful

They think I'm wonderful / Hey look who's wonderful / This corn-fed hick / Who said: "It might be keen / To build a town of green / And a wonderful road of yellow brick!"

See—I never had a family of my own—I was always travelin'. So, I guess I just wanted to give the citizens of Oz everything.

ELPHABA: So you lied to them.

WIZARD: Only verbally. Besides, they were the lies they wanted to hear!
The truth is not a thing of fact or reason / The truth is just what ev'ryone agrees on
Where I'm from, we believe all sorts of things that aren't true. We call it—"history."
A man's called a "traitor"—or "liberator" / A rich man's a "thief"—or "philanthropist" / Is one a "crusader"—or "ruthless invader?" / It's all in which label / Is able to persist / There are precious few at ease / With moral ambiguities / So we act as though they don't exist

They call me "wonderful" / So I *am* wonderful / In fact, it's so much who I am / It's part of my name / And with my help, you can be the same! / At long, long last receive your due— / Long overdue / Elphaba—the most celebrated / Are the rehabilitated / There'll be such a . . . whoop-de-doo / A celebration throughout Oz / That's all to do—with you . . .

Wonderful / They'll call you wonderful . . .

ELPHABA: It does sound wonderful . . .

WIZARD: Trust me—it's fun . . .

BOTH: When you are wonderful / It would be wonderful / Wonderful, wonderful—

WIZARD: One! Two! And . . .

He holds out his hand to her—she takes it and they dance together.

BOTH: We'll both be wonderful / Won't it be wonderful?

WIZARD: Once you too / Are a wonderful one!

ELPHABA: Wait!—I'll accept your proposition . . .

WIZARD: Wonderful!

ELPHABA: On one condition—

WIZARD: Yes?

ELPHABA: You set those Monkeys free . . .

WIZARD: Done!

He pulls the lever, the cage opens, and the winged Monkeys fly out of their prison. It's a joyful moment— until Elphaba discovers a familiar face, hidden beneath a blanket. It is her old friend Doctor Dillamond. She turns to the Wizard, furious at him and at herself for ever having trusted him.

ELPHABA: You and I have nothing in common. I'm nothing like you and I never will be. And I'll fight you till the day I die!

"I'LL ACCEPT YOUR PROPOSITION . . . ON ONE CONDITION: YOU SET THOSE MONKEYS FREE . . . ."

And with this, the Wizard immediately rushes behind his Giant Head.

WIZARD'S VOICE: Guards! Guards!

Two guards appear. Elphaba backs away from them, brandishing her broom, when she stops short: One of the guards is Fiyero.

    Glinda has heard the commotion and rushes to embrace her long-lost friend. But her relief turns to hurt and anger *when Fiyero declares his intention to leave—with Elphaba. Distraught, Glinda reveals to the Wizard and Morrible the one way to trap Elphaba: Get to her sister. As Morrible, a weather expert, cooks up a terrible storm, Glinda wanders off, sad and alone.*

GLINDA: Don't wish, don't start / Wishing only wounds the heart . . . /There's a girl I know / He loves her so / I'm not that girl . . .

CHAPTER XVI

Y A CAMPFIRE IN THE GREAT Gillikin Forest, Elphaba and Fiyero are alone at last . . .

ELPHABA: Kiss me too fiercely / Hold me too tight / I need help believing / You're with me tonight / My wildest dreamings / Could not foresee / Lying beside you / With you wanting me

Just for this moment / As long as you're mine / I've lost all resistance / And crossed some borderline / And if it turns out / It's over too fast / I'll make ev'ry last moment last / As long as you're mine . . .

FIYERO: Maybe I'm brainless / Maybe I'm wise / But you've got me seeing / Through different eyes / Somehow I've fallen / Under your spell / And somehow I'm feeling / It's "up" that I fell . . .

BOTH: Every moment / As long as you're mine / I'll wake up my body / And make up for lost time . . .

FIYERO: Say there's no future / For us as a pair . . .

BOTH: And though I may know / I don't care . . . / Just for this moment / As long as you're mine / Come be how you want to / And see how bright we shine / Borrow the moonlight / Until it is through / And know I'll be here holding you / As long as you're mine . . .

Fiyero studies her face.

FIYERO: What is it?

ELPHABA: It's just, for the first time—I feel wicked.

Elphaba hears a strange sound, then points to the sky, terrified.

ELPHABA: It doesn't make any sense. It's a house. But it's—flying through the sky! I have to go to Nessa!

CHAPTER XVII

T THE SITE OF THE CRASHED house in Munchkinland, Elphaba and Glinda confront each other. Both are equally devastated: Elphaba for the loss of her sister, Glinda for the loss of Fiyero.
    Fiyero arrives to protect Elphaba, allowing himself to be captured, so that Elphaba can save herself.

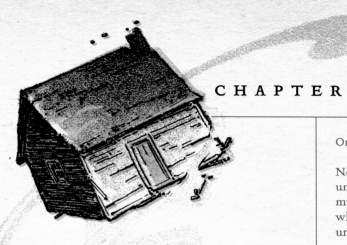

CHAPTER XVIII

T KIAMO KO CASTLE, ELPHABA chants a frantic spell in a desperate attempt to save Fiyero's life.

ELPHABA: Eleka nahmen nahmen / Ah tum ah tum eleka nahmen / Eleka nahmen nahmen / Ah tum ah tum eleka nahmen . . .

Let his flesh not be torn / Let his blood leave no stain / Though they beat him / Let him feel no pain / Let his bones never break / And however they try / To destroy him / Let him never die / Let him never die / Eleka nahmen nahmen / Ah tum ah tum eleka nahmen / Eleka nahmen nahmen / Ah tum ah tum eleka . . . Eleka . . . / What good is this chanting? / I don't even know what I'm reading / I don't even know what trick I ought to try / Fiyero, where are you? / Already dead or bleeding? /

One more disaster I can add to my / Generous supply?

No good deed goes unpunished / No act of charity goes unresented / No good deed goes unpunished / That's my new creed / My road of good intentions / Led where such roads always lead / No good deed / Goes unpunished . . .

Nessa . . . / Doctor Dillamond . . . / Fiyero . . . / Fiyero . . . !!

One question haunts and hurts / Too much, too much to mention / Was I really seeking good / Or just seeking attention? / Is that all good deeds are / When looked at with an ice-cold eye? / If that's all good deeds are / Maybe that's the reason why . . .

No good deed goes unpunished / All helpful urges should be circumvented / No good deed goes unpunished / Sure, I meant well— / Well, look at what "well-meant" did / All right, enough—so be it / So be it then / Let all Oz be agreed: / I'm wicked through and through / Since I can't succeed / Fiyero, saving you / I promise no good deed / Will I attempt to do / Again / Ever again / No good deed / Will I do / Again!

CHAPTER XIX

UTSIDE THE WIZARD'S PALACE, an angry mob has gathered. Morrible and Glinda observe them.

OZIANS: Go and hunt her / And find her / And kill her

A VICIOUS WOMAN: Good fortune witch hunters!

OZIANS: Go and hunt her / And find her / And kill her/ Wickedness must be punished / Evil effectively eliminated / Wickedness must be punished / Kill the Witch!

The Tin Woodman stands on a balcony above the crowd and addresses them fervently.

THE TIN WOODMAN: And this is more than just a service to the Wizard. I have a personal score to settle with Elph—with the Witch!
It's due to her I'm made of tin / Her spell made this occur / So for once I'm glad I'm heartless / I'll be heartless killing her!

ELPHABA AND GLINDA CONFRONT EACH OTHER. BOTH ARE EQUALLY DEVASTATED .

"LET ALL OZ BE AGREED: I'M WICKED THROUGH AND THROUGH . . . NO GOOD DEED WILL I DO AGAIN. "

THE TIN WOODMAN: You see—?
And the lion also / Has a grievance to repay / If she'd let him fight his own battles / When he was young / He wouldn't be a coward today!

CROWD: Kill her! Kill the Witch!

GLINDA: No—that's not how it happened! Madame— we've got to stop this, it's gone too far!

MORRIBLE: Oh, I think Elphaba can take care of herself.

ALL: Wickedness must be punished / Brave witch hunters, I would join you if I could / Because wickedness must be punished / Punished / Punished / But good!

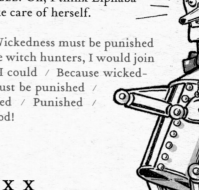

CHAPTER XX

ACK AT KIAMO KO CASTLE, GLINDA arrives unexpectedly. Elphaba demands that she leave, but Glinda refuses, begging Elphaba to surrender. One of the Monkeys flies in with a note . . . a note that takes the breath away from both girls.

GLINDA: It's Fiyero, isn't it? Is he . . . ?

ELPHABA: We've seen his face for the last time.

Elphaba realizes what must be done and asks Glinda to take over for her—to continue her work but never to try to clear her wicked name.

ELPHABA: Promise.

GLINDA: All right, I promise. But I don't understand.

ELPHABA: I'm limited / Just look at me—I'm limited / And just look at you— / You can do all I couldn't do, Glinda . . .

She gives Glinda The Grimmerie.

GLINDA: Elphie . . . You know I can't read this.

ELPHABA: Well, then—you'll have to learn.
Because now it's up to you / For both of us— / Now it's up to you

GLINDA: Oh, Elphie . . .

ELPHABA: You're the only friend I've ever had.

GLINDA: And I've had so many friends. But only one that mattered.
I've heard it said / That people come into our lives for a reason / Bringing something we must learn / And we are led / To those who help us most to grow / If we let them / And we help them in return / Well, I don't know if I believe that's true / But I know I'm who I am

today / Because I knew you . . .

Like a comet pulled from orbit / As it passes a sun / Like a stream that meets a boulder / Halfway through the wood / Who can say if I've been changed for the better? / But because I knew you / I have been changed for good . . .

ELPHABA: It well may be / That we will never meet again / In this lifetime / So let me say before we part / So much of me / Is made of what I learned from you / You'll be with me / Like a handprint on my heart / And now whatever way our stories end / I know you have re-written mine / By being my friend . . .

Like a ship blown from its mooring / By a wind off the sea / Like a seed dropped by a skybird / In a distant wood / Who can say if I've been changed for the better? / But because I knew you . . .

GLINDA: Because I knew you . . .

BOTH: Because I knew you / I have been changed / For good . . .

ELPHABA: And just to clear the air / I ask forgiveness / For the things I've done you blame me for

GLINDA: But then, I guess we know / There's blame to share

BOTH: And none of it seems to matter anymore

GLINDA:	ELPHABA:
Like a comet pulled from orbit	Like a ship blown off its mooring
As it passes a sun	By a wind off the sea
Like a stream that meets a	Like a seed dropped by
Boulder half-way Through the wood	a bird in the wood

BOTH: Who can say if I've been changed for the better? / I do believe I have been changed for the better

GLINDA: And because I knew you . . .

ELPHABA: Because I knew you . . .

BOTH: Because I knew you . . . / I have been changed for good.

The two friends embrace. And then . . . they hear the sound of footsteps.

ELPHABA: Hide yourself—!

THE CROWD: . . . And goodness knows / The wicked's lives are lonely / Goodness knows / The wicked die alone . . .

ELPHABA: Aaaahhhhh!

From her hiding place, Glinda witnesses what appears to be the melting of her friend. After the witch hunters have left, she picks up Elphaba's hat, and notices a small green bottle left behind.

CHAPTER XXI

 N THE WIZARD'S PRIVATE *chambers, Glinda makes a sudden and unexpected entrance.*

GLINDA: I've only seen a little green bottle like this one other time. And it was right here, in this room. You offered me a drink from it.

YOUNG WIZARD'S VOICE: Have another drink / My dark-eyed beauty . . .

WIZARD: Oh my lord— / I am a sentimental man / Who always longed to be / A father . . .

The Wizard sinks to his knees, heartbroken, realizing he has had his own daughter "liquidated."

GLINDA: I want you to leave Oz. I'll make the pronouncement myself: that the strains of Wizardship have been too much, and you're taking an indefinite—leave of absence. You'd better go get your balloon ready!

The Wizard stumbles off, a broken man, as Glinda turns to Madame Morrible.

Madame, have you ever considered how you'd fare? In captivity?

MORRIBLE: What? I don't—

GLINDA: Captivity. Pri-son.

She orders the guards to take Morrible away.

CELEBRANTS: Good news! She's dead! / The Witch of the West is dead! / The wickedest witch there ever was / The enemy of all of us here in Oz / Is dead!

No one mourns the wicked / Now at last she's dead and gone / Now at last there's joy throughout the land

GLINDA: Fellow Ozians. Friends . . . We have been through a frightening time. And there will be other times, and other things that frighten us. But if you'll let me, I'd like to try to help. I'd like to try to be—Glinda the Good.

CROWD: Good news! / Good news . . .

GLINDA: Who can say if I've been / Changed for the better / But . . .

ELPHABA AND GLINDA: Because I knew you . . .

CROWD: No one mourns the wicked . . .

GLINDA: Because I knew you . . .

ELPHABA AND GLINDA: I have been changed . . .

CROWD: No one mourns the wicked . . . / Wicked . . . / Wicked!

The End

"BECAUSE I KNEW YOU, I HAVE BEEN CHANGED FOR GOOD."

PLATE V.

IF SOMETHING BAD IS HAPPENING TO THE ANIMALS, SOMEONE'S GOT TO
TELL THE WIZARD. THAT'S WHY WE HAVE A WIZARD.

CHAPTER V

FOR GOOD

WE'VE SEEN HOW YEARS WENT IN THE PLANNING OF *WICKED*, the painstaking development of its music and libretto, the enormous efforts of its designers, and the creative crucible of the San Francisco tryouts. Producers Marc Platt and David Stone hired the best actors, designers, and director to turn Stephen Schwartz and Winnie Holzman's vision into a three-dimensional reality. The question remains: Why is *Wicked* such a hit? Fans, from young children to senior citizens, flock to the show, many for repeat viewings. In New York, advance ticket sales have topped $32 million, meaning it will run for years to come; it has a whirlwind 80-city national tour in progress and a "sit-down" or open-ended production in Chicago. As a critic, I've never seen a show with this much resonance and staying power. After picking the brains of the creative and producing team, a few tentative answers present themselves. First, *Wicked*'s themes operate on multiple levels at once: It is simultaneously a story of friendship and politics. Its themes stretch from the pecking order of school classrooms to the political machinations of national leaders. It is a skillful balance of comedy, tragedy, and morality tale. Psychologically, it's a very deft portrait of how a social pariah can internalize negativity and become transformed. It is a sophisticated view of how concepts like goodness and wickedness change meaning depending on who is speaking. And, of course, it is a testament to the transformative power of friendship. In part, the wonderful multiplicity and complexity of *Wicked*'s message is reflected in the variety of answers the cast and crew provided when asked: What makes *Wicked* so unique?

MARC PLATT: *Wicked* is an extremely satisfying experience for a bunch of reasons. It has accessible, tuneful music. It's full of the spectacle you would expect from the fantasy world of Oz. It tells a story of characters you walk into the theater thinking you know. Yet *Wicked* takes you to places you never expected, it twists and turns, and at the end of the evening, it moves you. Audiences laugh and applaud and cheer its sets, music, and costumes. But, at the end of the day, they leave the theater feeling different from when they walked in. Anytime you can do that—reading a novel, watching a film, seeing a play—people are going to say to everyone they know, "You've got to experience this."

DAVID STONE: We were advertising heavily and got a lot of press attention for the opening. But in retrospect, I think we didn't need to. *Wicked* took on a life of its own. The advertising helped create the image of a major hit. But the word of mouth was operating completely independently in selling tickets. When I have a flop, I can go down the list of things I did wrong. But when you have a hit, you sort of don't know what you did right. There's nothing specific. I can't tell what was right in our marketing beyond the fact that we conveyed our confidence about our show. People love the show. I was talking to another producer of a big Broadway hit, who said, "You know why *Wicked* is going to be a bigger hit than my show will? Because at musical comedies you have a great time, you tell people, 'That was a lot of fun.' And then you have dinner after. But ultimately people go to the theater to connect, to have big emotions. That's why *Wicked* is going to run longer."

BOB FENNELL (*Press Representative*): The critics were divided. But the fact of the matter is, positive reviews greatly outnumbered not-so-positive ones. Our national press was extremely good: *USA Today* and *Time* magazine. Also, high-profile media folks, like *Today* show host Katie Couric, loved the show. The

four women from *The View* came to the show and loved it. Ultimately, the most important thing is that audiences connected with it from the very beginning. You felt that at the first preview. My partner turned to me and said, "This is going to be a hit. I've had shows in this theater before. I have never seen a reaction like this. The audience loves this show. They're going to leave tonight and tell their friends they have to see it." And we saw it happen almost immediately. The numbers just kept increasing and increasing. At this point, two years after it opened, *Wicked* is stronger now, in terms of sales, than it has ever been. The demand is so great that people are buying tickets when they can get them. Every Broadway press agent hopes for a show that will continue to run and keep a lot of people employed for a long time. So it's very gratifying to walk into the Gershwin Theatre and see that it's sold out. I know people who have seen *Wicked* several times. And these are regular theatergoers, people who work in the industry. So, while cast changes can be difficult—and it's not easy finding people who can play these roles—there's something wonderful about that too. The cast keeps changing, but the show continues to be strong. And people come back to see the new people. It's fun.

STEPHEN SCHWARTZ: I never thought about whether or not it would be a hit, although one always hopes for that. I simply was trying to write what moved, excited, intrigued, and amused me. I think it would be presumptuous to try to speculate on how *Wicked* moved or excited other people. I can only say that I am thrilled that it has. Still, it's easy for a writer to say: "I don't think about other people's responses." It's not easy to do. I have never gotten a great deal of critical praise in my career, nor have I ever been highly regarded by the Broadway establishment. So to have a success like *Wicked* gives me renewed courage as a

writer to continue to trust my instincts. It helps me believe that if I just write, as honestly as I can and as well as I can, others will respond to it.

WINNIE HOLZMAN: It's about how we look at the world. Do we listen to what authority tells us? To me, that's what *Wicked* is about. In order to see what's really true, you have to engage something more than your judgment or your prejudices. You have to look with depth. I think that has social ramifications. It has political ramifications. And it has personal ramifications. Because it's about how we treat each other. Are we just seeing the outside? Or are we looking at people's hearts and souls, letting that enter our field of vision? The moment you start to do that, it's an incredibly freeing, exciting, exhilarating feeling. We can look at Elphaba and objectify her, as everyone in the plot is encouraging us to do—it's easy to do that. But you've missed the entire truth of her by doing that. That was what I had in mind a lot of the time when I was writing *Wicked*: What do we mean when we say the truth? Do we mean what we were told? Or what we've discovered? Can the truth just be told to you, and then you have it? No! People say different things for different reasons; it doesn't mean it's true. And they can parade it as truth, or they can disguise it as truth. But how do you find real truth? You have to dig.

JOE MANTELLO: When I first read the script, I remember thinking that if we all did our jobs, there was an audience for the show. When we were working on it, I would tell people, "It's about the Wicked Witch of the West and Glinda as young women, and they're roommates at school." Just hearing that, people would smile and say "I want to see that." So there was a built-in delight factor, even before Stephen and Winnie wrote one word. It's also such an emotional story. A lot of what's out there in the culture is ironic and comments on itself—that's fashionable right now. But there's something nice about *Wicked* being an old-fashioned musical comedy.

GREGORY MAGUIRE: I attended the *Wicked* CD release party, which was held in the Gershwin lobby in December 2003. The whole cast was there, except for Kristin, who had a cold. Stephen was there, signing copies of the album. I just sat on the stairs and watched a line of four or five hundred people slowly snaking along. Every fourteenth or so person getting their CD signed was a young woman between the ages of about 15 and 25. And many of them were women of color. There were a lot of Asian women and some Pakistani women wearing headscarves. Many of them just burst into tears. And Idina kept getting up out of her chair and leaning over the table awkwardly and hugging these young women, who looked at her and said, "You're the first person to demonstrate how I feel in my own life, how alone I feel, and how much I long to be empowered." I kept wiping my eyes. It was so wonderful. Even being halfway up the steps, watching it from a distance, I felt that I had done something good in writing *Wicked*.

KRISTIN CHENOWETH: I got to work with some fantastic people—particularly Winnie Holzman, she was the highlight. Also, I got close with a lot of the cast members because we went through everything together. I didn't know what kind of critical hit it would be, but I knew the audiences would love it. And that just warmed my heart to be in a show that audiences really loved. It was a wonderful ride and I will always look back on it with such fond memories. These days, I have got lots of great film opportunities. Like every actor, I want to move on and keep evolving and growing. I felt like I had done everything I could with Glinda. It was time to hang up the wand—or better yet, hand it off to someone else.

IDINA MENZEL: Being in the show affected me in so many ways. The biggest thing is that the character of Elphaba has reached out and touched so many people. I get responses on a daily basis from so many people—from five-year-olds to adults. It's been the most rewarding thing for me. I get letters saying how Elphaba helped people to embrace their power and their gifts in life. I think she's a great role model for young girls. I'm also proud that I got to work with that creative team. Just to sit in a room with Stephen and Winnie and Joe and Kristin. And it shows that hard work pays off. You know, I busted my butt! And I committed to this four years ago not knowing if it would ever make it to Broadway. I believed in my heart that there was something great about it—that *Wicked* was going to make a difference in the world.

FAN LETTERS

Fan letters pour in each day—to the cast, the creative team, and everyone involved in putting together the show. Some are funny and sweet, while others are downright moving. In the following pages, a few that stood out from the pack.

Farrah Abuzahria gave the following speech for the Theatre Development Fund's (TDF) Open Doors program graduation event on June 7, 2004, at Playwrights Horizons Theatre. Open Doors is a mentoring program for New York City high-school students that explores the relevance of theater to lives of today's youth.

Good Evening. My name is Farrah Abuzahria and I will be graduating from Midwood H.S. located in Brooklyn in just a couple of weeks. My mentors in my wonderful theater journey were Hal Prince and Kathleen Marshall. Both of them have had tremendous impact in shaping my Open Doors experiences and I'll be forever grateful for all that they have offered me.

I am Palestinian American Muslim, born and raised in Brooklyn, New York. My culture is very important to me. It gives me a sense of purpose and helps define who I am, yet it has also caused me a great deal of pain and hardship. Being Muslim and Arabic, I am faced with many different stereotypes, especially during this critical time in American history. I am labeled as a terrorist, and an immigrant, as well as other ignorant slurs. The portrayal of my people by the media only exacerbates the hatred that I am faced with on a daily basis. I can't understand why a piece of material can cause so much hatred.

I was very hesitant and nervous about going to the theater. I did not think I would fit into the theater crowd. I was weary about the stares that I would get for wearing my Muslim attire. I remember when I stepped into the theater for the first time and looked around, I was the only person who was wearing a scarf. I felt awkward and out of place, but what made things worse were the stares. Even my friend Nickisha was appalled at the stares that I received. Like me, she noticed them immediately. Yet despite my anxiety about sitting in an audience so different from me, everything changed the minute the lights went out and the curtain came up.

For the rest of my life, I will always remember my experience of seeing *Wicked*. I was brought to tears several times during the performance. I identified very strongly with the character of Elphaba. I felt all her emotions, from sadness to loneliness to defiance. I knew the pain she experienced as she was shunned for her green skin by her classmates. I, too, have been looked at as an outcast because of the scarf I choose to wear upon my head. I cried with her when she heard the horrible and untrue comments made about her. Her hardships paralleled the hardships and scrutiny I have had to endure. I never thought that my life could be portrayed up on stage, I never thought that the theater could move me as much as it has.

A major part of the Open Doors experience are the post-performance discussions. I've come to think of them as essential in making a difference in your life, yet I did not always feel this way. Like my initial experience of going to the theater, I was very anxious about speaking at the discussions. I felt intimidated about opening up and voicing my true opinions because I feared being rejected. I soon got over this, especially when I realized how down to earth and open-minded our mentors were. I became so comfortable talking to them that it felt like I was talking to friends. I also got a great deal from hearing the incredible insights that my other classmates had. The discussions were a safe place where diversity and tolerance for the views and beliefs of others was encouraged, not condemned.

Open Doors has opened a new life for me. Open Doors has given me confidence, I am able to step into the theater not worrying about the stares or glares. I am able to fully enjoy and appreciate the shows. I now know that I belong, and through the theater, I have found a new sense of hope for me and this world. Thank you.

Dear Mr. Schwartz,

I sincerely hope this letter reaches you. This is my first fan mail letter and I am in my forties, so that is saying a lot. I thank you so much for your work in *Wicked*. I have been a huge Broadway fan my whole life and this is my favorite show. I still listen to *Pippin* on a regular basis and have since the day I first got it. (I think I was 13?) I was fortunate to see the *Magic Show* and talked about it for a year. I also love *Pocahontas*.

I got to see *Wicked* recently and it will be an experience I will never forget. It was the best show I ever saw. The music held me from the first note. But, this is not the main reason for my letter. (Although this is a good enough reason.) I write to tell you of something much more amazing. As I stated earlier, I have been a Broadway fan my whole life. I have over 100 shows on CD. However, I married a man who can't stand the genre. (He has many other redeeming qualities.) We reached a compromise that I would only listen to my music when he is not around or while I am in my car.

We came to New York about a month ago and I dragged him to *Wicked*. He has seen other plays and can tolerate them and find good things to appreciate, but none of them ever really touched him.

Well, during Ms. Menzel's performance of "Defying Gravity," I look over and he had tears streaming down his face. I can't tell you what that meant to me.

I felt like Richard Gere in *Pretty Woman* during the opera scene. He insisted we get the soundtrack at the theater, did not want to take a chance that Tower Records would be out of it. He then played it over and over the next several days. Just recently I heard him confess to a good friend of his (another guy no less) that this is one of his favorite albums of all time. He still wells up with each listening.

You have brought so much joy to my life through your wonderful music. I think you are amazing. To see you open my husband's eyes to this world of musicals, well, it was truly astonishing. He said that this is what a musical should sound like. I agree. You have a rare gift and I thank you for sharing it with the rest of us.

You deserved the Tony. You won it in our heart.

Thank you.

Yours very truly,
JENNIFER H.

Good Day

This summer our daughter, Margaret, got the opportunity to visit New York and see *Wicked* with her Grammie. I cannot begin to tell you the wonderful impact the show made on my daughter's life.

She is a quiet, loving, sensitive 10 (almost 11) year old who shows very little excitement for anything. She's rather reserved when it comes to most things. One must take her word for it when she says she likes something or is having a good time, because it could not be guessed by merely looking at her. Then she came home from New York and spent an entire evening telling her dad and me all about *Wicked*! Her eyes would light up, and she would laugh about some things, and get excited about others! Two months later, it is still her favorite CD and subject to talk about. (I'm excited for her to get a little older to tackle the book by Mr. Maguire.)

This very brief synopsis of the wonderful impact the show has made on our daughter brings me to the point of writing this letter.

Each year for Christmas we give her a special ornament representing something about her year. I would very much like to fill a glass ornament with some pieces of fabric, trim, ribbon, buttons, or whatever from the costumes from the show *Wicked*. I know this may seem like an unusual request, but I am asking anyway. If the answer is, "Yes, of course, we'd be happy to do that for her!", I've enclosed a SASE. If by chance the answer is a very sad, "No," you may throw the envelope out. Regardless, I thank you for your time reading this. And I thank you further for being part of such a magical show that made a great impact on our daughter!

With much appreciation,

KATIE V.
ST. LOUIS, MO

Dear the cast and crew of *Wicked*,

I wasn't really sure where to mail this letter but this was the only address I could find. I hope this gets to the right people.

I am writing this letter to thank you, all of those involved with the production of *Wicked*. It was amazing. The set was the best I've ever seen. The vocals were so amazing that during intermission I rushed to get the CD and have been listening to it since. The show made me cry not only because of the plot itself but also because of how much it related to my life and what I've been through. It became very special to me and I will never forget seeing the show for the first time and I plan on seeing it again soon.

Two years ago, when I entered high school, I gave up my dream of becoming a dancer. When I began dancing four years ago, I wanted nothing more than to become a dancer and attend NYU after high school. When I entered high school, I still loved to dance but I became more "realistic" and thought that dance wasn't something that would be a "sure thing" so I shouldn't waste my time with it after high school—I should go to college for something more realistic. So I developed a desire to become an English teacher. It felt right, so naturally my focus shifted and dance and theater continued to be something I did on the side.

A few months ago, in June, I had my last dance recital. Next year I won't be able to take dance classes because I have to get a job and also because of my junior course load. I've only danced for four years but they have been the best years and I have come a long way. Before seeing the show, I again felt unsure of what I wanted to do after high school. Being a teacher just didn't seem right anymore. I wanted more out of life. More of taking chances and living life how I want to and not how I should, according to others. Then I saw *Wicked* and everything changed. I guess I should thank Idina Menzel also because she sang "Defying Gravity" so well and when she sang that song, I had tears in my eyes. I realized that I could give up weekly dance classes but not dance altogether. I've been dancing in NYC for three years and I can't give up my dream to be a dancer. Who knows where this dream will lead me, but I will never know if I don't at least try. That song and her performance of it gave me the strength to try again and this time I'm not giving up. When I think about it, it all feels so right. I love to dance and I love to sing more than anything. It was said in the movie *Flashdance*, "You give up your dream, you die," and that is true. I am not going to give up.

I can't express how good and right this feels. I also can't express my gratitude for this show coming to Broadway. It has had such an unexpected effect on my life and it makes me smile just thinking about it. Thank you so much and to everyone involved with the show, keep up the good work. I look forward to seeing the show again soon.

All my love and best wishes,
ALIX C.
CHESHIRE, CT

P.S. AS SOMEONE ONCE SAID, "IT IS SOMETIMES WISER TO FOLLOW THE DREAMS OF YOUR HEART THAN THE LOGIC OF YOUR MIND." I AM NOW TO FOLLOW MY HEART . . .

OZIAN TRAVELOGUE

VISITING OZ FOR THAT WELL-EARNED VACATION? OR JUST SURVIVED A CYCLONE? HERE ARE SOME FAVORITE TOURIST ATTRACTIONS...

KIAMO KO CASTLE
IN WINKIE COUNTRY

DON'T MISS

Guided tours will lead visitors through the castle, with special attention paid to the sleeping quarters for Chistery and the Flying Monkeys, Dorothy's cell, and the infamous water pail that destroyed the Wicked Witch.

SHOPPING

Stop by the Kiamo Ko Gift Shop on your way out to purchase a commemorative mini-bucket or a wind-up Flying Monkey doll!

ALSO

Some say the Wicked Witch didn't really go to her watery grave at the hands of Dorothy. Search the castle floors for hidden trapdoors that may tell another story.

CAR **365** SEAT **12B**

the EMERALD CITY

DON'T MISS

Wizomania, the theatrical extravaganza, tells how the Wonderful Wizard came to Oz; it features song-and-dance routines by the delightful Flatheads.

SHOPPING

The Emerald City denizens are quite the fashion mavens. And don't forget your green spectacles!

ALSO

Being the center of culture of Oz, it has a plethora of museums, galleries, and restaurants to visit.

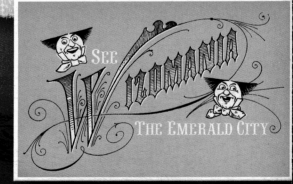

See **WIZOMANIA** THE EMERALD CITY

UPPER UPLANDS
of Gillikin

DON'T MISS
This picturesque northern region is home to Glinda the Good. The area boasts some of the nicest homes (and wealthiest estates) in Oz.

SHOPPING
The best in life is here, but it doesn't come cheap!

ALSO
Sure, people here may be a bit focused on looks and social status, but they certainly know goodness when they see it.

CAR **122**　SEAT **08A**

Shiz University
IN OZ WE TRUST

DON'T MISS
Ozdust Ballroom. Shiz University students are notorious for their hedonism as well as their mental acumen.

SHOPPING
Shiz Boutique. Mix and match from a dizzying assortment of vests, dresses, ties, and sweaters—all with the unmistakable Shiz blue-and-white pattern.

ALSO
The sharpest minds of Oz flock to this august institution to hone their academic and magical skills. And party, of course. Sit in on a history class or brush up on your sorcery skills.

CAR **667**　SEAT **13C**

MUNCHKINLAND

DON'T MISS
See the birthplace of the Wicked Witch of the West, also the Governor's Mansion where the Wicked Witch of the East ruled with an iron fist.

SHOPPING
The area is mostly agrarian and not terribly commercialized, but the Munchkinland Gift Shop includes some attractive garden gnomes and T-shirts that say, "A Kansas Farmhouse Landed on Me and All I Got Was this Lousy T-shirt"

ALSO
You can search the countryside for the remnants of Dorothy's Farmhouse.

CAR **724**　SEAT **02F**

OZIAN GLOSSARARIUM

Getting around Oz can be confusifying—if not outright horrendible—if you don't have the proper maps or a handy phrasebook. This indispensable glossararium will help you sling the lingo of the realm as easily as a Munchkin. Armed with the knowledge of Oz's common expressions and popular places, you can charm a Winkie Prince, swap hairstyling tips with the beautiful people of the Upper Uplands, or be a whiz on the quiz at Shiz. As Galinda sings, "I'll help you be popular! You'll hang with the right cohorts, you'll be good at sports, know the slang you've got to know . . ."

ROOT LANGUAGE ABBREVIATIONS

AOD = ANCIENT OZIAN DIALECT [mostly obsolete]

NMO = NEW MODERNIST OZIAN [typically spoken around Emerald City and Shiz University]

UO = UNIVERSAL OZIAN [the lingua franca of Oz, perfectly intelligible from East to West and North to South]

———

BATTERING RAMIKIN \ *n* [BAT-er-ing RAM-uk-kin; AOD origins unknown, possibly modification of kitchen implements dragooned for martial purposes, such as a large container for cake mix] An instrument used to break down doors, esp. in pursuit of uppity sorceresses. (*ActISc14*)

BRAVERISM \ *n* [BRAV-er-ism; AOD bravo! Meaning "better you than me."] Quality of courage, often lacking in lions and Wonderful Wizards, that can reach raving proportions. (*ActIISc1*)

CLANDESTINEDLY \ *adv* [clan-DESTINED-lee; UO term from clan or family, and destined or meant to be] Secretly, on tiptoes, to avoid being caught. (*ActISc7*)

CONFUSIFYING \ *adj* [con-PHEW-zuh-fie-ing; back formation from AOD conphew, obsolete term for the sound of a head being scratched] Being so perplexing and unfathomable, one must turn to a handy Ozian Glossararium for a definition. (*ActISc1*)

CONGRATULOTIONS \ *n* [cun-grach-you-LO-shuns; UO combined form of ancient congrats, small rodents prone to effusive praise, and u-lotion, Ozian skin-care product] A somewhat unctuous form of public approval. (*ActIISc1*)

DECIPHERATE \ *v* [duh-SY-fer-ate; AOD obsolete term for reading ancient runes and natural phenomena, predating the Clock of the Time Dragon] To be able to read and thereby cast a spell. (*ActISc13*)

DEFINISH \ *adj* [DEAF-innish; AOD derived from feh, old Ozian expression of ambivalence] Equivocatory affirmation, falling between definite and not so definite; useful in empty promises made by sinister headmistresses. (*ActISc2*)

DEGREENIFY \ *v* [De-GREEN-if-eye; NMO] To bleach of all verdant hues; a magic spell that even the greatest Wizard couldn't cast. (*ActISc2*)

DEMANDERATING \ *adj* [duh-MAND-er-ating; NMO] Doubly difficult, esp. in terms of witchcraft. (*ActISc4*)

DESPONDIARY \ *adj* [de-SPON-dee-airy; AOD from despondree = depressed diary] A condition of being in the dumps so much that you fill your diary with awful doodles of black storm clouds and frowning faces. A terrible affliction that can strike witches both wicked and good. (*ActIISc9*)

DEVASTRATED \ *adj* [DEV-uh-stray-ted; NMO] Made to feel very sad. (*ActISc9*)

DISCOVERATE \ *v* [dis-COV-er-ate; NMO derived from AOD discos, secret meeting places for Ozian dance fanatics, banned by the Wizard] To reveal in a highly dramatic fashion. (*ActIISc3*)

DISGUSTICIFIED \ *adj* [dis-GUST-tiss-e-fied; UO derived from AOD dissing someone with gusto] A state of being beyond grossed out, usually by green-skinned roommates. (*ActISc3*)

DISRESPECTATION \ *n* [dis-ree-speck-TAY-shun; UO] Insult that comes as a surprise, undermining one's expectations. (*ActIISc3*)

DISTURBERANCE \ *n* [dis-TURB-er-ants; from NMO nonce-term for the picnic-ruining Disturber Ants, commonly found in lower Munchkinland] Loud or upsetting hubbub, esp. caused by unruly Shiz University students. (*ActISc4*)

ENCOURAGERIZE \ *v* [en-CUR-ridge-er-ize; UO from AOD for curs, or brave mutts] To imbue with bravery; esp.

applicable to Munchkinlanders and Cowardly Lions. (*ActISc6*)

FESTIVATING \ *v* [FEST-uh-vay-ting; UO] To party raucously and with reckless abandon. Usually done after the melting or crushing of witches [see rejoicify]. (*ActIISc9*)

GALINDAFIED \ *adj* [Guh-LIN-da-fied; NMO early name of Glinda] 1. Undergoing a makeover process that became incredibly popular after the demise of the Wicked Witch of the West. 2. Made to look pretty and perfect, sometimes at the expense of one's true feelings. (*ActISc8*)

GRATITUTION \ *n* [grat-ih-TOO-shun; NMO expression of thanks so strong, the speaker makes up a word on the spot] Feeling of thankfulness. (*ActISc6*)

THE GRIMMERIE \ *n* [GRIM-er-ee; AOD from ancient mythology] Also known as the Ancient Book of Thaumaturgy and Enchantments. The tome of spells first used by Elphaba, subsequently bequeathed to Glinda. *See* Gregory Maguire's Introduction, page 1.

HIDEOTEOUS \ *adj* [hid-ee-OH-tee-us; UO orig. coinage from Shiz students shopping in the school store] So offensive to the eye, it's just plain odious. Commonly applied to pointy black hats way out of fashion that only a crazy Wicked Witch might wear. (*ActISc6*)

HORRENDIBLE \ *adj* [hor-REND-ih-bull; UO] So horrible one doesn't know whether to tear it up or eat it. A slander sometimes directed to magic books of spells. (*ActIISc2*)

LINGUIFICATION \ *n* [LING-whiff-feh-cajun; NMO academic jargon] 1. A field of study, principally taught at Shiz University, that involves the thrilling pursuit of philology: etymology, usage, and neologism. (Really, it is very excitifying!) 2. The least popular classes at Shiz (darn sorcery!). (*ActISc2*)

MANIFESTORIUM \ *n* [man-uh-fest-OR-ee-um; UO derived from an infestation of strange manners] Outward sign or indication of something innate. Tricky word to use with absolute certainty, since interior and exterior don't always match up. (*ActISc14*)

MOODIFIED \ *adj* [MOO-duh-fied; UO from depressed cows] Grumpy, melancholic, and given to unpredictable swings in attitude. Often seen in Winkie Princes when they discover they've fallen in love with green girls. (*ActISc10*)

OUTUENDO \ *n* [OUT-you-end-oh; NMO extension of out, you! a colloquial exclamation at hearing some really juicy gossip] Rumormongering that's even more insidious and outrageous than innuendo—if you know what I mean (wink, wink!). (*ActISc1*)

OZMOPOLITAN \ *adj* [oz-mah-PAUL-ittan; NMO used in urban centers mostly by snobs] 1. Term of utmost trendiness, especially used by Emerald City dwellers to indicate up-to-the-minute niftiness and worldliness. 2. Term of disparagement for Ozians in less developed parts of the country, denoting pretentiousness and snootiness. But what do those boobs know? (*ActISc12*)

REJOICIFY \ *v* [re-JOYCE-if-eye; UO origin of Joyce unclear; maybe a friend of Dorothy?] Celebrate not once, but several times; typically after the death of a Wicked Witch, with much group singing and dancing. (*ActISc1*)

SCANDALACIOUS \ *adj* [scan-duh-LAY-shus; UO for delectable misbehavior] So bad it's good! Strangely enough, the term is positive when applied to bad-boy Winkie Princes, but negative when applied to a Wicked Witch. (*ActISc5*)

SURREPTITIALLY \ *adv* [sir-rep-TISH-uh-lee; NMO onomatopoeic construction from the sound of Munchkinlanders moving about quietly: "surrep, surrep…"] In a manner marked by sneakiness that may or may not involve sneakers. (*ActIISc1*)

SWANKIFIED \ *adj* [SWANK-uh-fied; AOD from the ancient Swanks, a northern people marked by their impeccable taste in clothing and well-appointed houses] 1. Made to look fancier or cooler than it actually is. 2. Gussied-up, like a green-skinned Witch with a pointy hat. (*ActIISc5*)

THRILLIFYING \ *adj* [THRILL-uh-fy-ing; UO] Very exciting, for example learning that you're about the meet the Wizard of Oz. (*ActISc9*)

WICKEDEST \ *adj* [WIK-uh-dissed; NMO wiccen + dissed; insult sorceress] 1. Superlative form of "wicked," denotes a state of utmost badness or malevolency. 2. Among some more advanced thinkers, following the demise of the Wicked Witch of the West, it became a term indicating coolness or intensity. (*ActISc1*)

WIZOMANIAC \ *n* [whiz-oh-MAIN-ee-ack; NMO from Emerald City showbiz] Die-hard fan of *Wizomania,* the smash hit Emerald City extravaganza about the Wonderful Wizard of Oz; some Wiz-o-maniacs have been known to see the show a dozen times! (Where do they get the money?) They are also to be found mobbing the stage door for the performers. (*ActISc12*)

Credits and Acknowledgments

TEXT CREDITS:

All text by David Cote, except: courtesy of John Fricke: 10–13 (written with David Cote); © 2003 Winnie Holzman: 38 (note cards); © 2003 Winnie Holzman 140–177 (abridged story for "Songs and Story of *Wicked*"); © 2005 Gregory Maguire: 1; © 1995 Gregory Maguire : 40–41 (original manuscript of *Wicked: The Life and Times of the Wicked Witch of the West*); © 2005 Gregory Maguire and Wicked LLC: 19, 20, 21, 31, 35, 73, 182 (Gregory Maguire interviews only); courtesy of Marc Platt: 23 (note cards); © 2003 Stephen Schwartz: 82–4 (lyrics and music of "Defying Gravity"); © 2003 Stephen Schwartz: 140–177 (lyrics and music for "Songs and Story of *Wicked*"); courtesy Farrah Abuzahria: 184

ILLUSTRATION/ARTWORK

W. W. Denslow: 5, 10–13, 26, 70, 76, 79, 80, 85, 92 (top), 138, 140, 143, 152, 155, 159 (top), 164–6, 171, 175; Susan Hilferty: 122–7 (all costume sketches); Headcase Design: 2, 16, 32, 67, 74, 88, 139, 150, 159 (bottom), 178, 188–9; Kelly Holohan of Holohan Design: 37, 72, and 132–3; Eugene Lee: 96–7, 100–1, 103 (top), 104–5; © 1993 Gregory Maguire, 39; Sean McCabe 141–2, 145, 148–9, 151, 153, 156–7, 158, 160, 162–3, 168–9, 172–3, 174, 177; John R. Neill: 3, 34, 50, 92 (bottom), 161, 176, 183, 186; *Playbill*: 181; book cover illustration © 1995 Douglas Smith, for *Wicked: The Life and Times of the Wicked Witch of the West*, © 1995 Gregory Maguire, HarperCollins Publishers: 19

PHOTOGRAPHY CREDITS:

All photography by Joan Marcus, except: © 1998 Constance Brown: 91 (top) photograph for *The New Yorker*; © Dan Bigelow/Getty Images: 15 ; courtesy Winnie Holzman: 180; © 2003 Henry Leutwyler: 8 (photograph originally published in *Vanity Fair*), 53, 54, 57, 58, 61; © 1999 Andy Newman: 21; courtesy of Marc Platt: 20; courtesy of Serino-Coyne Inc.: Cover illustration and billboard design (180)

TIMELINE:

Photo editing and research by John Fricke: 10–11 (by year): 1882, photograph of L. Frank Baum, from Fricke collection; 1891, photograph of Baum with his family, from the late Matilda Jewell Gage, courtesy The Matilda Joslyn Gage Foundation; 1910, photograph of L. Frank Baum, from the late Matilda Jewell Gage, courtesy The Matilda Joslyn Gage Foundation; 1919, photograph of L. Frank Baum, © Bettmann/CORBIS ca. 1890s

12–13 (by year): 1939, photograph of Judy Garland and Mickey Rooney, from Fricke collection; 1956, photograph of Liza Minnelli and Lorna Luft, from Fricke collection; 1957, courtesy of the International Oz Club; 1973, © 1975 Bettmann/CORBIS (photograph of Elton John); 1995, *Wicked: The Life and Times of the Wicked Witch of the West*, © 1995 Gregory Maguire, HarperCollins Publishers, book cover illustration © 1995 Douglas Smith: 12; 2004, courtesy of *Playbill*; 2004, © 2003 Bruce Glikas (photograph of David Stone with Idina Menzel)

PHOTOGRAPHY IDENTIFICATIONS:

68 (from left) Kristin Chenoweth and Idina Menzel, Original Broadway Cast
69 (from left) Kristin Chenoweth and Idina Menzel, Original Broadway Cast

76 (from left) Original Broadway Cast; Christopher Fitzgerald, Kristin Chenoweth, and Original Broadway Cast
77 (from left) Idina Menzel, Original Broadway Cast; Logan Lipton and Ensemble, Original Tour Cast
78 (from left) William Youmans, Original Broadway Cast; Jennifer Laura Thompson and Joey McIntyre, Broadway Cast; Idina Menzel and Kristin Chenoweth, Original Broadway Cast
79 (from left) Stephanie J. Block, Original Tour Cast; Jennifer Laura Thompson, Idina Menzel, and the Broadway Cast
80 (from left) Joel Grey, Original Broadway Cast; Stephanie J. Block, Original Tour Cast
85 (from left) Carol Kane, Kendra Kassebaum, and Ensemble, Original Tour Cast; Stephanie J. Block and David Garrison, Original Tour Cast
86 (from left) Kendra Kassebaum, Original Tour Cast; Norbert Leo Butz and Idina Menzel, Original Broadway Cast; Idina Menzel, Original Broadway Cast; Ensemble, Original Tour Cast
87 (from left) Idina Menzel and Kristin Chenoweth, Original Broadway Cast; Kendra Kassebaum, Original Tour Cast
93 Ensemble, Original Broadway Cast
103 Bob Keller
114 Patrick Gilmore and Tommy Gloven
115 Adinah Alexander and George Hearn, Broadway Cast, with Joseph Schwarz
122 Stephanie J. Block, Original Tour Cast
123 Kristin Chenoweth, Original Broadway Cast
124 Peter John Chursin, Original Tour Cast
125 Carol Kane, Original Tour Cast
126 Christopher Fitzgerald and Kathy Deitch, Original Broadway Cast
127 Matt Clemons and Katie Adams, Original Tour Cast
132–3 Stephanie J. Block, Original Tour Cast, and Joseph Dulude II.
135 Ensemble, Original Broadway Cast
137 Stephanie J. Block, Original Tour Cast
141 Jennifer Laura Thompson, Broadway Cast
142 Barbara Tirrell and Lori Holmes, Original Tour Cast
145 Idina Menzel and Carole Shelley, Original Broadway Cast
148–9 William Youmans, Original Broadway Cast
151 Idina Menzel, Original Broadway Cast
153 Kendra Kassebaum, Original Tour Cast
157–8 Kristin Chenoweth and Idina Menzel, Original Broadway Cast
160 Stephanie J. Block, Original Tour Cast
162–3 Stephanie J. Block and Ensemble, Original Tour Cast
165 Carol Kane, Kendra Kassebaum, and Ensemble, Original Tour Cast
166 Shoshana Bean, Broadway Cast
167 George Hearn, Broadway Cast
168–9 Stephanie J. Block and Ensemble, Original Tour Cast
170 Norbert Leo Butz and Idina Menzel, Original Broadway Cast
172–3 Kristin Chenoweth and Idina Menzel, Original Broadway Cast
174 Idina Menzel, Original Broadway Cast
177 Kendra Kassebaum, Original Tour Cast

ACKNOWLEDGMENTS:

A HUGE THANKS TO THE FOLLOWING PEOPLE WHO HELPED TO MAKE *WICKED*: *THE GRIMMERIE* ALMOST AS "WONDERFUL" AS *WICKED* THE MUSICAL:

Marc Platt, Joey Levy, Chris Kuhl, Cindy Chang, and Bette Einbinder; David Stone; the team at 321 Theatrical Management, especially Nancy Gibbs, Susan Sampliner, Laura Kirspel, and Marcia Goldberg; the amazing publicity team, Bob Fennell and Molly Haydon; Robert Miller and Hyperion, including Ellen Archer, Beth Dickey, Charlie Davidson, Zareen Jaffery, Sharon Kitter, Michael Rentas, Will Schwalbe, and Deirdre Smerillo; the incredible Winnie Holzman, Gregory Maguire, Joe Mantello, and Stephen Schwartz; the team at Melcher Media, including David Brown, Lauren Nathan, Lia Ronnen, Lindsey Stanberry, and Megan Worman; and everyone else who helped change this book "For Good": The Araca Group, Mark Andrews, Loretta Bussen, Michael Cole, Nina Essman, Elin Flack, Max Goldstein, Bess Marie Glorioso, Kristen Harris, Richard Hester, Chris Jamros, Brooke Lee, Rick Miramontez, John Moses, Judith Regan, Carmen Sanchez, Meighan Stoops, Alex Tart, Sally Wagner, Anna Wahrman, and—of course—the entire cast and crew of *Wicked*.

A VERY SPECIAL THANKS TO THE UNIVERSAL TEAM THAT SUPPORTED *WICKED* FROM THE VERY BEGINNING:

Ron Meyer, Stacey Snider, Scott Stuber, Holly Bario, Romy Kaufman, Jimmy Horowitz, Keith Blau, and Universal Pictures.

BIOS:

DAVID COTE is the theater editor and chief drama critic for *Time Out New York*. He has also reviewed television, books, and movies for the magazine. He is a contributing critic on NY1's *On Stage* TV program. In *The New York Times*, *Opera News,* and *Maxim*, he covered diverse topics such as contemporary radio drama, operatic staging, and forensics. Throughout the 1990s, he performed in and directed many avant-garde theatrical productions Off-Off Broadway. His career in journalism began by editing and publishing his own 'zine—*OFF: a journal of alternative theater*. B.A. Bard College, 1992.

JOAN MARCUS is a theatrical photographer working in New York today. After serving as the in-house photographer at the Kennedy Center in Washington D.C. for many years, Joan has photographed literally hundreds of productions and artists both onstage and in her studio over the past two decades.

PAUL KEPPLE and JUDE BUFFUM are better known as HEADCASE DESIGN, an award-winning graphic design and illustration studio based in Philadelphia. Their work has been recognized by such publications as the *AIGA's 365* and *50 Books/50 Covers*, *American Illustration*, *Communication Arts*, and *Print*.

This book was produced by MELCHER MEDIA, INC. 124 West 13th Street, New York, NY 10011 www.melcher.com

Publisher: CHARLES MELCHER
Associate Publisher: BONNIE ELDON
Editor in Chief: DUNCAN BOCK
Editor: HOLLY ROTHMAN
Production Director: ANDREA HIRSH
Editorial Assistant: SHOSHANA THALER

Marc Platt, Universal Pictures, The Araca Group, Jon B. Platt and David Stone

present

WICKED

Music and Lyrics by Stephen Schwartz • Book by Winnie Holzman • Based on the novel by Gregory Maguire
Directed by Joe Mantello • Musical Staging by Wayne Cilento
Orchestrations by William David Brohn • Music Director Stephen Oremus
Settings by Eugene Lee • Costumes by Susan Hilferty • Lighting by Kenneth Posner • Sound by Tony Meola
Projections by Elaine J. McCarthy • Wigs & Hair by Tom Watson
Music Arrangements by Alex Lacamoire & Stephen Oremus • Dance Arrangements by James Lynn Abbott • Music Coordinator Michael Keller
Associate Set Designer Edward Pierce • Special Effects by Chic Silber • Flying Sequences by Paul Rubin/ZFX Inc.
Production Supervisor Steven Beckler • Technical Supervisor Jake Bell • Assistant Director Lisa Leguillou
Casting Bernard Telsey Casting CSA; Bernie Telsey, Wil Cantler, David Vaccari, Bethany Knox, Craig Burns, Tiffany Little Canfield
Marketing TMG The Marketing Group • Executive Producers Marcia Goldberg & Nina Essman
General Management 321 Theatrical Management; Nina Essman, Nancy Gibbs, Marcia Goldberg
General Press Representative The Publicity Office; Bob Fennell, Marc Thibodeau, Michael S. Borowski

Assistant to Mr. Schwartz	Michael Cole
Assistants to the Producers	Joey Levy, Patrick Catullo, James Pellechi, Terrie Lootens Parella
Assistant Scenic Designer	Armond D. Francone
Oz Map Design	Francis Keeping
Set Model Construction	Miranda Hardy, Lauren Alvarez
Associate Costume Designers	Michael Sharpe, Kenneth Mooney
Assistant Costume Designers	Maiko Matsushima, Amanda Whidden, Amy Clark
Mask Design	Matthew W. Mungle
Make up Design	Joseph Dulude II
Associate Lighting Designers	Karen Spahn, Warren F. Flynn
Assistant Lighting Designers	Ben Stanton, Aaron Spivey
Associate Sound Designer	Kai Harada
Assistant Sound Designers	Shannon Slaton, Adam Rigby
Projection Programmers	Mark Gilmore, Hillary Knox
Assistant Projection Designers	Jenny Lee, Michael Patterson, Jacob Daniel Pinholster
Projection Animators	Gareth Smith, Ari Sachter Zeltzer
Special Effects Associate	Aaron Waitz
Associate Hair Designer	Charles LaPointe
Fight Director	Tom Schall
Production Carpenter	Rick Howard
Production Electrician	Robert Fehribach
Production Propertyman	George Wagner
Synthesizer Programming	Andrew Barrett for Lionella Productions, Ltd.
Legal Counsel	Loeb & Loeb/Seth Gelblum
Legal Counsel for Universal Pictures	Keith Blau

	ORIGINAL BROADWAY COMPANY	ORIGINAL FIRST NATIONAL TOUR COMPANY
Cast	Kristin Chenoweth & Idina Menzel, Carole Shelley, Norbert Leo Butz, Michelle Federer, Christopher Fitzgerald, William Youmans with Adinah Alexander, Ioana Alfonso, Ben Cameron, Cristy Candler, Kristy Cates, Melissa Bell Chait, Marcus Choi, Kristoffer Cusick, Kathy Deitch, Eden Espinosa, Melissa Fahn, Rhett G. George, Kristen Leigh Gorski, Manuel Herrera, Kisha Howard, LJ Jellison, Eddie Korbich, Sean McCourt, Corinne McFadden, Mark Myars, Jan Neuberger, Walter Winston ONeil, Andrew Palermo, Andy Pellick, Michael Seelbach, Lorna Ventura, Derrick Williams and Joel Grey as the Wizard	Stephanie J. Block & Kendra Kassebaum, Jenna Leigh Green, Logan Lipton, Timothy Britten Parker, Derrick Williams with Katie Adams, Aaron J. Albano, Timothy George Anderson, Terra Lynn Arrington, Peter John Chursin, Matt Clemons, Nicolas Dromard, Laura Dysarczyk, Maria Eberline, Brooke Elliott, Lori Holmes, Adam Lambert, K.W. Miller, Kristen F. Oei, Chris Peluso, Don Richard, Emily Rozek, Christopher Russo, Brian Slaman, James Tabeek, Barbara Tirrell, Brooke Wendle, Nicole Winhoffer, and Carol Kane and David Garrison
Company Manager	Susan Sampliner	Mark Andrews
Production Stage Manager	Steven Beckler	Richard Hester
Stage Manager	Erica Schwartz	Maximo Torres
Assistant Stage Managers	Chris Jamros, Bess Marie Glorioso	Timothy R. Semon
Dance Captains	Mark Myars, Kristen Leigh Gorski	James Tabeek
Assistant Choreographer	Corinne McFadden	Mark Myars
Associate Company Manager	Barbara Crompton	Laura Kirspel
Head Carpenter	C. Mark Overton	Matt Biltgen
Automation Carpenter	William Breidenbach	Henry Baker
Head Electrician	Pat Gilmore	Brendan Quigley
Assistant Electricians	Brendan Quigley, Valerie Gilmore	Jacob Martin, Richard Tatum
Properties	Joe Schwarz	Trevor Ricci, Kyle Barrineau
Production Soundman	Douglas Graves	Douglas Graves
Assistant Sound Engineer	Jack Babin	Michael Weferling
Production Wardrobe Supervisor	Alyce Gilbert	Stacey Stephens
Assistant Wardrobe Supervisor	Dennis Paver, Kristine Bellerud	Mary Seasly, Randy Werdal
Hair Supervisor	Alfonso Annotto	Lisa Thomas
Assistant Hair Supervisor	Chris Clark	Andrea DiVincenzo
Music Preparation Supervisor	Peter R. Miller, Miller Music Service	Anixter Rice Music Services
Conductor	Stephen Oremus	Robert Billig
Associate Conductor	Alex Lacamoire	Dominick Amendum
Musicians	Christian Hebel, Victor Schultz, Kevin Roy, Danny Miller, Laura Sherman, Jon Owens, Tom Hoyt, Dale Kirkland, Douglas Purviance, Helen Campo, Tuck Lee, John Moses, John Campo, Theo Primis, Kelly Dent, Gary Seligson, Konrad Adderley, David Evans, Paul Loesel, Ric Molina, Greg Skaff, Andy Jones	Paul Masse, Chuck Pierce, Matt VanderEnde

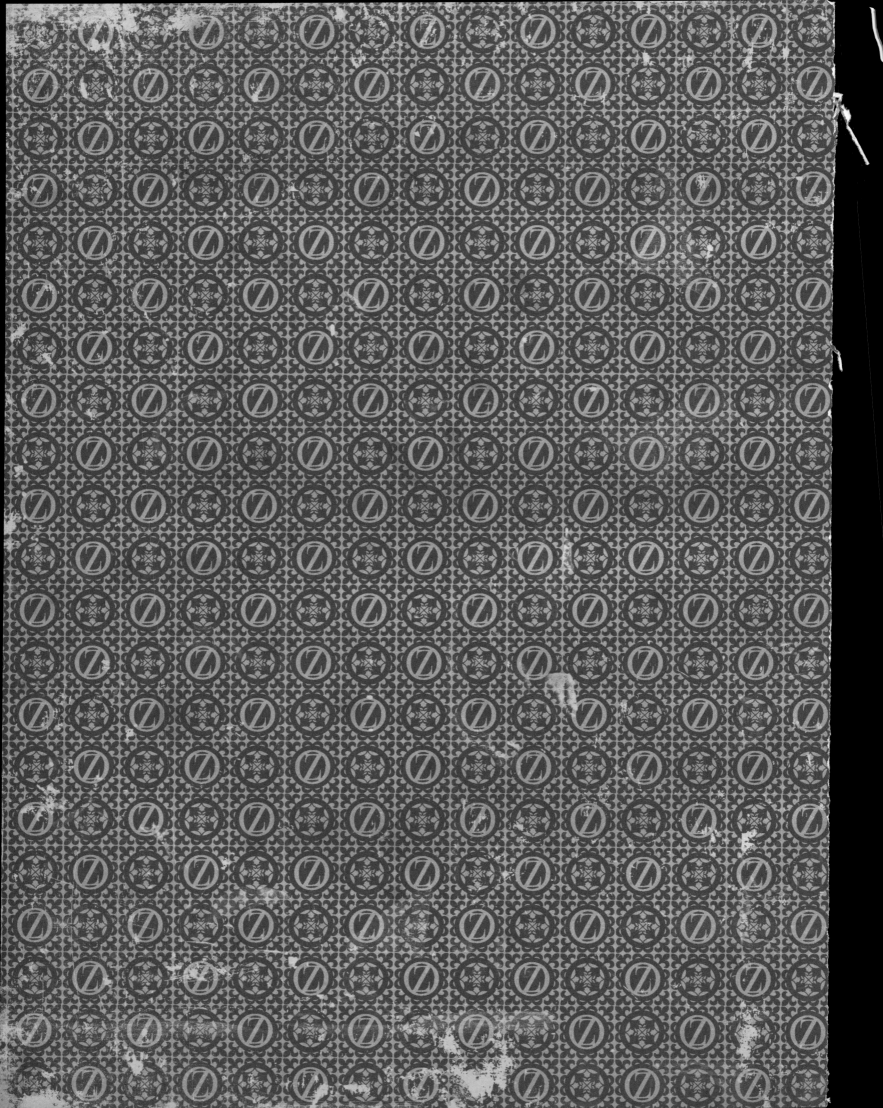